SHARED FLAVORS

A GROUP OF FRIENDS SHARING THEIR FAVORITE RECIPES

By Shared Cookbook 2012 Authors

Mediterranean Food - Eva Pleuhs
Side Dishes to Make Your Dinner Party an Event - Joan Ryan
White Pozole - Laura Cramer
Fondue with Friends - Geri Sorenson, Holly Bates and Michele Murphy
A Ladies Lunch - Nanette Kelley and Mary Pacchini
Super Easy Recipes - Sharon Taylor and Lyn Crosby
Thanksgiving Sides - Mariette Kaplan and Family
All Crepes - Teresa Abascal
Traditional Jewish Dinners - Lauren Margolin
Mexican Fiesta – Rosy Hugener
The Greek Kitchen -Mia Psaltis Connolly, Christina Galanis Angelos, Eva
Skordilis, Julie Kokonis Phipps, Mary Panagakis, Georgene Karkazis Shanley,
Constance Gekas Hugdahl, Alexandra Vainikos Carson and Dimitra Alexakos
Favorite Recipes. Margaritas. - Sara McKinnon Martinez and Anya Martinez
Recipes from Xnipec Restaurant-Maria Luisa Romo
Vicki's Holiday Traditions – Vicki Peterson

Shared Cookbook

Copyright © 2012 by Shared Cookbook 2012 Authors
Mediterranean - Food-Eva Pleuhs
Side Dishes to Make Your Dinner Party an Event- Joan Ryan
White Pozole – Laura Cramer
Fondue with Friends - Geri Sorenson –Holly Bates – Michele Murphy
A Ladies Lunch - Nanette Kelley and Mary Pacchini
Super Easy Recipes- Sharon Taylor and Lyn Crosby
Kaplan's Thanksgiving Sides –Mariette Kaplan
All Crepes - Teresa Abascal
Traditional Jewish Dinner - Lauren Margolin
Mexican Fiesta – Rosy Hugener
The Greek Kitchen -Mia Psaltis Connolly, Christina Galanis Angelos, Eva Skordilis, Julie Kokonis Phipps, Mary Panagakis, Georgene Karkazis Shanley, Constance Gekas Hugdahl, Alexandra Vainikos Carson and Dimitra Alexakos
Favorite Recipes - Sara McKinnon Martinez and Anya Martinez
Recipes from Xnipec Restaurant-Maria Luisa Romo
Vicki's Holiday Traditions– Vicki Peterson,

This book was published by Shared Pen
SHARED PEN Edition
www.SharedPen.com
ISBN:978-1481050364
Library of congress Number:

For information about the book go to
www.sharedcookbook.com

EASY TO FIND RECIPES COLOR CODE

	Vegetarian		Chicken/Turkey
	Side Dish		Pork/Lamb
	Beef		Fish/Sea
	Pasta		Appetizer
	Main dish		Soup
	Salad		Dessert
	Breakfast		Snacks/Drinks

> *What I've enjoyed most, though, is meeting people who have a real interest in food and sharing ideas with them. Good food is a global thing and I find that there is always something new and amazing to learn - I love it!*
>
> **Jamie Oliver**

> If you really want to make a friend, go to someone's house and eat with him... the people who give you their food give you their heart.
>
> **Cesar Chavez**

TABLE OF CONTENTS

MEDITERRANEAN FOOD-EVA PLEUHS

Mediterranean food consists mainly of fresh fruits and vegetables, pasta, grains, rice, seafood and poultry. Grilling or broiling is the preferred method of cooking and olive oil is the most frequently used fat. Yogurt and cheese also play an important role in the Mediterranean kitchen

Hi, my name is Eva - I am originally from Germany but have lived in the United States for almost a decade. I absolutely love to cook and experiment in the kitchen, which I think I inherited from my mother. While I was growing up, we had a garden with plenty of fruits and vegetables that had to be harvested, cooked and preserved. My mom was the designated cook but I was allowed to experiment as much as I wanted to in the kitchen.

My family always loved to travel, which cultivated my love for Mediterranean food. When I was younger, we often traveled to former Yugoslavia. The food there was incredibly rich and tasty! As I loved food, I tried absolutely everything there. Since then, I have also traveled to Italy, France and Spain, and realized that the food there is equally delicious, but much lighter from what I had experienced previously.

My family and I have been vacationing in Northern Spain every summer for almost 20 years now, and the food and restaurants there are absolutely my favorite. I fell in love with the country, the people and the wonderful food and every time we spend time in Spain I only cook local dishes that do not require a lot of effort, only need a few ingredients, but taste great!

When I am in Spain, I love to visit the farmers markets. The smell and taste of the fresh produce is incredible and once you realize how much better it tastes than what you can buy at the grocery store, you never want to buy your produce anywhere else again. The people are so friendly, and if you tell them you are making a certain dish, they will help you handpick the right ingredients. .

The dishes that I shared with you in this book are easy to prepare, do not take a lot of effort and taste absolutely great. They are best prepared with ingredients that are very fresh and of the best quality you can find.

PASTA WITH ARUGULA, ZUCCHINI, TOMATOES AND FETA

- 1 lb spaghetti
- 16 oz / 450 g cherry tomatoes, cut in half
- 2 small or medium zucchinis (3.5 – 4 cups or about 1 lb) , cut in 1/2 inch – 1 inch dices
- 7 oz / 200 g / feta, crumbled or diced
- 1/2 bag of arugula (you will need about a small hand full per person)
- 2 - 3 tablespoons good olive oil, plus extra for drizzle over the dish
- optional: black olives
- salt, pepper

This is a super easy to prepare meal that is quick and flavorful.

Hot Pasta is tossed with briefly cooked zucchinis and just melted tomatoes.

The dish is finished with aromatic Greek feta and served over fresh arugula. It couldn't be easier.

1. Cook the pasta according to the package instructions in salted water until al dente.

2. In the meantime take out some nice big plates. Scatter a hand full of the arugula onto the plates.

3. 4 Minutes before the pasta is done heat a pan over med-high to high heat and add 2 Tablespoons of the olive oil. Add the zucchini and cook them for about 2 - 3 minutes, you don't want them too soft, they should still have a little crunch.

4. Right before you drain the pasta, add the halved tomatoes to the pan and let them melt, not longer than a minute.

5. Season the vegetables with salt and pepper, then add the drained pasta to the pan.

6. Mix everything carefully and serve it over the arugula. Scatter the feta over the pasta, drizzle with some extra olive oil and serve

FAVA BEAN SALAD

Serves four as an appetizer

- 3.5 / 100 g oz bacon
- 15.5 oz / 450 g baby fava beans, fresh or frozen
- 3 tomatoes, roughly chopped
- 1 teaspoon or more sherry or red wine vinegar
- 1 tablespoon balsamic vinegar
- 1 - 2 tablespoons olive oil
- 3 tablespoons chopped parsley
- salt and freshly ground pepper

It is funny how taste can changes over the years, right?

I didn't care much for fava beans when I was younger. My mother used to cook them in a stew that was served over potatoes. This was the only dish I ever had that used fava beans as an ingredient. When I tasted these beans the first time in a salad I fell in love with them.

Conveniently, they are available frozen, so that you can enjoy them all year round. If you can't find fava beans you can replace them with Edamame.

1. Heat one teaspoon of olive oil in a frying pan over medium heat. Add the diced bacon and cook until it starts to get golden brown. Add the onion and cook the mixture until crisp and brown. Put on a plate lined with paper towels and put aside. Discard almost all the fat in the pan.

2. Add the beans to the now empty pan, add a little bit of water and 1 teaspoon of salt. Cover and cook until the beans are almost done. This can vary depending on your beans but usually only takes a couple of minutes. Drain the beans when they are done. Put them back in the pan and add 1 Tablespoon of balsamic vinegar, let cool slightly. Put the tomatoes in a bowl and add the slightly cooled beans to the tomatoes. Add the rest of the olive oil and 1 teaspoon red vine vinegar and taste with salt and pepper. Serve with parsley and the bacon / onion mixture.

PASTA WITH OLIVES, TUNA AND ROASTED RED PEPPER

In the heat of the summer cold pasta sauces are a great way to serve a light and satisfying dish without putting in too much effort. This dish combines sweet roasted red peppers, olives and tuna. This pasta dish is easy to make and absolutely fabulous. You can use the above measurements as a guideline but you can use as much or as little of the ingredients as you like. Just taste and let your taste buds guide you.

- *130 ml / 4.5 oz olive oil or more*
- *1 can of roasted red peppers, cut into stripes (about 200 g / 7 oz) (use piquillo peppers if you can find them)*
- *1 can of the best quality canned tuna you can afford (about 250 g / 8.8 oz)*
- *1 cup / 150 g green olives, halved*
- *juice of 1 – 2 lemons*
- *salt and pepper*
- *a handful of basil or parsley, chopped*
- *1 pound pasta*

1. Cook the pasta according to the package instructions, until al dente. In the meantime put the peppers into a bowl. Add the tuna and the olives. Add the olive oil and lemon juice and mix carefully. Taste with salt and pepper.

2. When the pasta is cooked, drain it. Put the pasta back into the pot and mix carefully with the sauce. If the dish seems too dry add more olive oil to loosen it up. Taste and adjust the seasoning. Sprinkle with the herbs and serve immediately.

3. Cooked, drain it. Put the pasta back into the pot and mix carefully with the sauce. If the dish seems too dry add more olive oil to loosen it up. Taste and adjust the seasoning. Sprinkle with the herbs and serve immediately.

MEDITERRANEAN OMELET WITH GRILLED EGGPLANT

Serves four as an appetizer or two as an main dish

Tasty, flavor filled omelets are a great way to enjoy the vegetables that are in season. This version contains grilled eggplant, black olives and goat cheese. Enjoy this dish for breakfast, lunch or dinner.

- *1 medium eggplant (about 14 oz / 400 g)*
- *¼ cup / 1.4 oz / 40 g of black olives, pitted and halved*
- *2.8 oz / 80 g goat cheese*
- *2 small handful of arugula*
- *olive oil*
- *salt and pepper*
- *6 large eggs*
- *2 tablespoons of milk*
- *1 tablespoon of pine nuts, toasted (optional)*

Note: if using an 8 inch pan this will make two generous omelets and should be made in two batches. If your pan is bigger you can make one big omelet out of this recipe.

1. Line a baking tray with paper towels.
2. Cut the eggplant (horizontally or diagonally) in slices, no bigger than ¼ inch (1cm). Put on paper towels and sprinkle generously with salt. Wait 5 minutes, then turn over and sprinkle the other side with salt. Let sit for approx 30 minutes and then dry them off thoroughly.
3. Heat a griddle or grill pan to medium high heat. Brush the pan with a little olive oil and grill the eggplant on both sides until evenly charred and soft - just a couple of minutes. You might have to do this in two batches.
4. When they are nicely charred and soft put on a plate and brush with a little olive oil on one side. Season with pepper and salt and set aside.
5. This can be prepared a day in advance.
6. Heat a nonstick pan to medium heat and add 1 teaspoon of olive oil.
7. Beat the egg lightly with the milk and season with salt and pepper. Pour the mixture in the pan and arrange the eggplants (brushed with olive oil side on top) on top of the eggs. Sprinkle the olives around the eggplants and cover with a lid. Let cook until the omelet is just set.
8. Alternatively, you can cook the omelet for 2 minutes and finish it in the oven under the broiler for a couple of minutes. 9. Slide the omelet on a plate, sprinkle the goat cheese, arugula and pine nuts on top and serve hot or warm. ne nuts on top and serve hot or warm.

PIE WITH OVEN DRIED TOMATOES AND EGGPLANT

Serves four as an appetizer

Filling (can be made a day ahead)

- 1 eggplant, cut in ½ inch / 1 cm inch slices
- 1 handful of grated parmesan
- 2 lb / 1 kg tomatoes
- olive oil
- salt and pepper
- 1 tablespoon sugar
- a couple slices of mozzarella
- 3 tablespoons chopped herbs (rosemary, thyme, oregano, marjoram, chives)
- basil for garnish

It is very easy to dry tomatoes in the oven yourself. They are softer than commercial sun-dried tomatoes, with a delicate, rich and sweet flavor. You can use them for all sorts of dishes. Serve them with mozzarella, goat cheese or feta, add them to a salad or add them to pasta. I decided to put them on a tart and also added eggplants and a lot of Mediterranean herbs. This tart needs some time but it is mostly hands-off time and can be prepared in advance. The tomatoes will need at least two hours to dry, so plan accordingly. The crust is super buttery, crunchy and flaky.

Make the filling

1. Preheat your oven to 425 F. Line a baking pan with aluminum foil and brush lightly with olive oil. Arrange your eggplant slices on the pan, season with salt and pepper, brush with more olive oil and bake until soft and golden 15 – 20 minutes, turning the eggplants once halfway through.

For the Pastry (can be made a day ahead)

- 1 ¼ / 165 g cup all-purpose flour, chilled in the freezer for 30 minutes
- ¼ teaspoon salt
- 4 oz / 115 g cold butter, cut into ½ inch dices and chilled in the fridge again
- ¼ cup / 60 g sour cream
- 2 teaspoons lime or lemon juice (fresh)
- ¼ cup / 60 ml ice water
- 1 egg yolk beaten with 1 teaspoon water

2. Drop the temperature of your oven to 250 F /120 C.

In the meantime put your tomatoes in a bowl and pour some boiling water over them. Let them sit for 30 seconds. Cut in half take the skin off and gently press the liquid and seeds out of your tomatoes.

3. Line another baking pan with aluminum foil (or the same one if the eggplant is done) and brush with olive oil.

4. Arrange the tomatoes with the cut side down onto the baking sheet. Season with salt and pepper and sprinkle the sugar evenly over the tomatoes. Let them dry in the oven for about 2 hours for about 2 hours.

Make the pastry

1. Mix the sour cream, ice water and lemon juice in a small bowl. Put back in the fridge.

2. Take the flour out of the freezer and mix in a medium bowl with the salt. Add the cubed butter pieces and with your fingers or a pastry blender mix until the mixture looks like coarse meal.

3. Add the liquid and mix until it forms into dough. Don't over mix. It is ok to see some bigger pieces of butter and lumps.

4. Press into a flat disk, wrap in foil and refrigerate for 1 hour.

Assembling.

1. Preheat your oven to 400 F / 200 C

2. Roll the dough to a 12 – 14 inch circle. The easiest way to do this is to roll it between floured baking paper or cling wrap

3. Sprinkle the parmesan in the middle of the dough.

4. Arrange the eggplant slices, leaving a 2-inch border on the dough. Sprinkle with half of the herbs. Put the dried tomatoes on the eggplant. Sprinkle with more herbs. Arrange the mozzarella slices on the vegetables and season with salt and pepper. Fold the edges of the dough over the filling. You want a rustic look here. Brush the border with the egg yolk. **5.** Bake for approx. 30 minutes until the crust is golden brown and the filling bubbly.

6. Let cool for some minutes and garnish with the basil. Serve hot, warm or at room temperature.

COLD MELON SOUP

Serves four as an appetizer

- 1 – 2 cantaloupe or gallia melon
- juice of ½ lemon
- 2 tablespoons of orange juice
- 1/8 teaspoon cayenne pepper
- ¾ t kosher salt
- salt and pepper
- 12 small shrimp for serving
- olive oil
- aleppo or chile pepper
- a couple of mint or basil leaves or both

A cold gazpacho is the best way to cool down on a hot summer day. It is light and refreshing, yet bursting with summer flavor.

The sweetness of the melon blends wonderfully with the spiciness of the cayenne pepper. You can add a tablespoon of cream if you like the soup creamier and less spicy. It is best to let the soup rest in the fridge for a couple of hours or better yet over night; that way, all the flavors have time to unfold.

let the soup rest in the fridge for a couple of hours or better yet over night; that way, all the flavors have time to unfold.

1..Put the first six ingredients in a blender. Blend until smooth. Taste and adjust the seasoning.

2..Put in the refrigerator for a couple of hours or best overnight. Heat a pan with a tablespoon of olive oil. When the oil is hot add the Aleppo or Chile pepper and then the shrimp. Cook until the shrimp are pink and done. When they are cool enough to handle, skewer the shrimp on a stick. Taste the soup again and adjust the seasoning. Garnish with the basil or mint leaves and serve with the shrimp.

MEDITERRANEAN TOMATO SAUCE FOR SEAFOOD

Serves four

This is my favorite tomato sauce for any dish you make with seafood. There are so many recipes out there, like Marcella Hazan's simple tomato sauce for pasta or Jamie Oliver's tomato sauce for pizza, but this recipe is truly perfect when paired with seafood. The addition of fennel seeds and saffron makes it develop a taste that is similar to that of paella or a bouillabaisse. Truly Mediterranean!

- 1.5 kg / 3 lb tomatoes,
- 300 g / 10.6 oz onions (2 medium), peeled and cut into ½ inch / 1cm dices.
- 1 pinch of saffron
- ½ - 2 teaspoons of sweet or picant spanish paprika (start with ½ teaspoon and add more if you like it more spicy)
- 1/2 teaspoon of dried estragon
- 1/2 teaspoon of anis or fennel seeds
- 2 small dried chili peppers or a pinch of cayenne or chili powder
- 1 tablespoon of aceto balsamico
- ½ - 1 teaspoon sugar
- 4 teaspoon of olive oil
- 1 tablespoon of butter
- salt and pepper to taste

1. Peel the tomatoes. The easiest way to do this is to put them in a bowl and pour some boiling water over the tomatoes. Do not let them sit longer than 30 seconds.

2. Drain and rinse with cold water. Then core, peel and chop roughly. Heat the olive oil in a pan over medium heat. Add the onions with a pinch of salt and let them cook while stirring every now and then for about 3 to 4 minutes until soft and golden. Grind the spices (saffron, anis or fennel, estragon, chili peppers) in a pestle and mortar and add the spices to the onions. Add the Spanish paprika.

3. Let the spices cook no longer than 30 seconds then add the tomatoes, sugar, the balsamico and the butter. Let the sauce simmer with the lid on over low heat for approximately 15 minutes. If the sauce seems too thin, let it reduce for another 10 minutes. Taste with salt, pepper and sugar. Add the seafood and let it cook until done.

4. Serve with good rustic bread or over pasta.

ROASTED PEACHES WITH BISCOTTI CRUMBLE

- *5 biscotti cookies (about 1 ounce / 30 g total)*
- *3 tablespoons walnuts,*
- *2 tablespoons whole wheat flour*
- *1 tablespoons brown sugar*
- *1.5 oz / 40 g butter, melted*
- *2 firm but ripe large peaches, rinsed, wiped clean of fuzz, halved, pitted*
- *Vanilla ice cream*

This is a classic Italian dessert, easy to prepare and absolutely delicious. The ripe fruit is stuffed with a biscotti cookie mixture and then baked until nicely browned and soft.

Serve with vanilla ice cream or vanilla sauce.

1. Preheat the oven to 350 F / 180 C
2. Grease a baking pan that is big enough to hold the fruits comfortably with butter.
3. Arrange the prepared fruit in the pan.
4. Put the cookies in a plastic bag and smash them with a heavy rolling pin.
5. Put in a bowl. Add the chopped walnuts, the flour, sugar and melted butter and mix.
6. Fill the mixture in the peaches and bake for approximately 20 minutes or until soft and golden brown.
7. Serve with vanilla ice cream

SIDE DISHES TO MAKE YOUR DINNER PARTY AN EVENT- JOAN RYAN

GRATINEE OF CAULIFLOWER

6- 8 portions

- 6 tablespoons unsalted butter
- 4 cloves garlic, minced
- 4 ounces thinly sliced prosciutto, cut into thin strips
- Florets of 1 large head cauliflower, cut into ¼ inch lengthwise slides
- 2 tablespoons unbleached all-purpose flour
- 1-1/2 cups heavy or whipping cream
- Pinch cayenne pepper
- Salt and freshly ground black pepper, to taste
- 1-1/2 cups grated gruyere or swiss cheese

1. Preheat oven to 350 degrees.
2. Melt butter in a large skillet over medium heat. Add the garlic and sauté 2 minutes. Stir in the prosciutto and sauté 2 minutes more.
3. Add the cauliflower and cook just until it begins to lose its crispness, 3 or 4 minutes.
4. Stir in the flour and then the cream. Blend well. Season with the cayenne and salt and pepper to taste. Heat to boiling and immediately remove from heat.
5. Pour the cauliflower into a shallow au gratin dish. Top with the cheese and parsley. Bake until the top is lightly browned and bubbling, about 30 minutes. Serve immediately.

- 1/2 ounce dried porcini mushrooms
- 1 quart vegetable broth
- 1 1/2 cups cracked farro or barley
- 2 tablespoons extra virgin olive oil
- 1/2 cup onions, finely chopped
- 1 lb. cremini mushrooms or 1 lb. wild mushrooms, cleaned, trimmed and sliced
- salt
- 2 garlic cloves, minced
- 2 teaspoons fresh rosemary, chopped
- 1/2 cup dry white wine
- 1/3 cup parmesan cheese, grated
- 1/4 cup fresh parsley, chopped

MUSHROOM FARRO RISOTTO

8 portions

1. Place the farro in a bowl, and pour on enough hot water to cover by an inch. Let soak according to package instructions (some types of farro must be soaked overnight).

2. Place the dried mushrooms in a large bowl. Cover with 2 cups boiling water. Let sit 30 minutes.

3. Drain the mushrooms through a strainer set over a bowl and lined with a paper towel. Squeeze the mushrooms over the strainer, then rinse in several changes of water to remove grit. Chop coarsely. Set aside.

4. Add the broth from the mushrooms to the stock. You should have 6 cups (add water if necessary). Place in a saucepan, and bring to a simmer. Salt to taste.

5. Heat oil over medium heat in a large skillet. Add the onion, stir until it begins to soften, about three minutes.

6. Add the fresh mushrooms. Cook, stirring, until they begin to soften and sweat. Add salt to taste, garlic and rosemary. Continue to cook, stirring often, until the mushrooms are tender, about five minutes.

7. Add the farro and dried mushrooms. Cook, stirring, until the grains of farro are separate and beginning to crackle, about two minutes.
Stir in the wine until absorbed.

8. Add all but about 1 cup of the stock, and bring to a simmer. Cover and simmer until the farro is tender, about 50 minutes. Remove the lid, and stir vigorously from time to time. Taste and adjust seasoning.

9. There should be some liquid remaining in the pot but not too much. If the farro is submerged in stock, raise the heat and cook until there is just enough to moisten the grains, like a sauce. If there is not, stir in the remaining stock. Add the Parmesan, parsley and fresh ground pepper to taste, and stir together. Remove from the heat and serve.

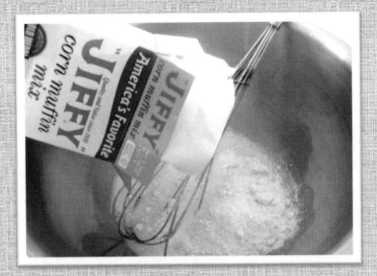

FRAN RYAN'S CORN PUDDING

8 portions

- 1 (17 oz.) can whole kernel corn
- 1 (17 oz.) can cream style corn
- 1 stick butter, melted and cooled
- 1 (8 oz.) pkg. sour cream
- 2 eggs, beaten
- 1 pkg. Jiffy corn muffin mix

1. Beat eggs.
2. Add melted, cooled butter
3. Add sour cream, corn, and Jiffy mix.
4. Put into 2 1/2 quart casserole.
5. Bake about 1 hour at 350 degrees or until the top is crispy and brown

Note: Can be doubled for a crowd, and back in a 9" x 13" pan. For a spicier dish, add one can of green chili's (drained).

- *1 pound dry spaghetti*
- *2 tablespoons extra-virgin olive oil*
- *4 ounces pancetta or slab bacon, cubed or sliced into small strips*
- *4 garlic cloves, finely chopped*
- *2 large eggs*
- *1 cup freshly grated Parmigiano*
- *Reggiano, plus more for serving*
- *Freshly ground black pepper*
- *1 handful fresh flat-leaf parsley, chopped*

SPAGHETTI CARBONARA

4 – 6 servings

1. Prepare the sauce while the pasta is cooking to ensure that the spaghetti will be hot and ready when the sauce is finished; it is very important that the pasta is hot when adding the egg mixture, so that the heat of the pasta cooks the raw eggs in the sauce.

2. Bring a large pot of salted water to a boil, add the pasta and cook for 8 to 10 minutes or until tender yet firm (as they say in Italian "al dente.")

3. Drain the pasta well, reserving 1/2 cup of the starchy cooking water to use in the sauce if you wish.

Meanwhile, heat the olive oil in a deep skillet over medium flame.

4. Add the pancetta and sauté for about 3 minutes, until the bacon is crisp and the fat is rendered.

Toss the garlic into the fat and sauté for less than 1 minute to soften.

5. Add the hot, drained spaghetti to the pan and toss for 2 minutes to coat the strands in the bacon fat.

6. Beat the eggs and Parmesan together in a mixing bowl, stirring well to prevent lumps. Remove the pan from the heat and pour the egg/cheese mixture into the pasta, whisking quickly until the eggs thicken, but do not scramble (this is done off the heat to ensure this does not happen.)

7. Thin out the sauce with a bit of the reserved pasta water, until it reaches desired consistency.

8. Season the carbonara with several turns of freshly ground black pepper and taste for salt.

9. Mound the spaghetti carbonara into warm serving bowls and garnish with chopped parsley. Pass more cheese around the table.

WILD RICE AND CRANBERRY PILAF

3 servings, 1 cup each

- *1 pkg. (5.9 oz.) near East Garlic and Herb Long Grain and Wild Rice*
- *1 – 14.5 oz. low sodium, fat free chicken broth*
- *¼ cup sunflower seeds*
- *¼ cup dried cranberries*
- *¼ cup raisins or currants*
- *1/3 cup almonds*
- *3 green onions, sliced*

1. Prepare Near East rice according to package directions, except use chicken broth instead of water.
2. Stir in sunflower seeds, cranberries, raisins, green onions, and almonds and serve.

WHITE POZOLE – LAURA CRAMER

"White Pozole" is a hearty Mexican soup traditionally made with pork, hominy and seasonings. It's served with a wide array of toppings. Hominy is one of the main ingredients of pozole, which is basically processed corn. As many know, corn was a sacred plant for the Aztecs.

White Pozole became popular in the southern state of Guerrero. In fact, every Thursday in most of the state, it's called Pozole night.

It's common to find this dish at parties since it can be prepared in large amounts to satisfy many guests. Mexican people celebrate special occasions with Pozole.

My favorite pozole is the white kind in honor of my deceased mother, who used to make the world's best White Pozole for our birthdays!

WHITE POZOLE

Ingredients for the broth:

- 2 pounds pork leg, cut into stew-size chunks
- 2 pounds pork neck bones (for extra broth flavor)
- 1 large can of hominy
- 1 medium head of garlic, separated and peeled
- 1/8 of a cup of coriander seeds
- 1 medium onion cut it into four parts
- Salt and pepper
- Enough water to cover pork

Toppings:

- 1 onion chopped
- 5 limes sliced
- Dried oregano
- Piquin Chile (powder)
- 12 Corn tostadas
- 3 avocados, Sliced
- 3 serrano chiles (chopped)
- ½ of shredded lettuce head
- 8 sliced radishes

1. - Open the hominy can, drain, rinse and set aside.

2. – Bring water to a boil, and add the meat, onion, salt and pepper as needed.

3. - Meanwhile, mash garlic with coriander seeds in a mortar. Add the mixture through a coriander to the broth. Let it simmer.

4. - Once the meat is tender, take it out and shred it.

5. - Lastly, add the hominy and shredded meat to the broth.

Serve it hot in a bowl and add as many toppings as you like. Accompany it with tostadas.
Provecho = Bon Appetite!!!

FONDUE WITH FRIENDS - HOLLY BATES, MICHELE MURPHY AND GERI SORENSON

I have grown up watching my mother entertain crowds of 2 and crowds of 100 and developed a love for entertaining friends and family!

I love to try new things and watch our guests faces as they taste each meal or laugh and smile while they share stories with other good friends and family members. Entertaining at home is how we express gratitude for friendship, celebrate special occasions, and continue family traditions.

20 years ago I dug out my mother's old avocado green fondue pot and invited some friends over for what turned out to be a fun and memorable evening that eventually developed into a tradition that our 3 kids kids and close friends look forward to as a highlight of our holiday season.-**Holly Bates**

Over the years, the tradition of gathering with family in Green Bay has congregated around food. This was usually done in the format of a pot luck where everyone would bring a dish of their choice.

Fondue can work similarly where each person can contribute in their own way by choosing their favorite entree, dip or sauce and is one of the least complicated ways to entertain. Everyone took a part and contributed. It made the "sharing" one of the strongest elements and successes! Be it the sharing of recipes, foods, stories or gifts it's our shared lives that web together and make each celebration special.

If we (Geri, Holly and I) have to travel hundreds of miles or just down the street, we will find a way. It's our friendship that is most important. The "good eats" are just a bonus, while the collaboration during the preparation and the joy of sharing it is what makes it truly special.- **Michele Murphy**

I was born and raised in Green Bay, WI, but have lived in Illinois for over 20 years. As a little girl, I remember those endless hours spent creating recipes with my easy bake oven. I'd invite my friends over to enjoy my easy cakes and cookies. We would spend hours eating and pretending to dine like our parents did. Entertaining started at a very young age for me. Some of my fondest memories are family fondue meals. My family would spend hours eating one piece at a time while laughing and reminiscing of funny stories. I have carried this family tradition to my children and it has now become one of our cherished traditions. New Years is the crescendo, where we enjoy a fun filled night with family and friends - huddled around pots of fondue.- **Geri Sorenson**

INTRODUCTION TO FONDUE

For decades, fondue has been a family tradition in homes all over the USA. For us, it has been a New Year's Eve tradition for adults and kids as far back as the kids can remember. What could be more fun than a meal with dozens of different flavors to suit everyone while good friends and family gather for hours of laughter and wine?

What started out as a Swiss dish lead to expansion to the US in the 1960's. Many of us recall our parents' avocado green and harvest orange fondue pots heated by tins of sterno. Today you can find electric fondue pots and the likes of Williams and Sonoma and Crate and Barrel made of stainless steel on lazy susans. Whatever the history of your pot, we think fondue should be a part of your meal making repertoire.

For the first timers, fondue might seem overwhelming. What do we cook? What dips do we use? Do I need special plates? How do we prepare the food? Well, you can relax! This could be one of the easiest yet, most memorable dinners you have ever made!

- Choose your favorite recipes.
- Delegate the shopping lists!
- Set up your table.
- Prep your food and platters.

Have the cheese course in a ceramic pot to avoid burning. You can have it all in the pot ready to heat in the microwave right before you sit down.

In the metal pots, we suggest you use peanut oil, as it does not "smoke" like other oils do. You will need to preheat this on the stove before putting it on the table.

For the chocolate course, you should again use a ceramic pot and you can have everything ready in the pot to melt right before you enter the desert course.

Set out one platter for your cheese items (breads, grapes, apples, etc.), one for your main course (shrimp, lobster, beef, chicken) and one for your deserts. As guests arrive, you can place their items right on the platter and throw away the bag. (No worrying about washing dishes and returning them later!)

You will want to set up small dishes for the dipping sauces. You can line them on a long platter or place them around the lazy Susan if you have one.

SHOPPING LIST

Meats, Poultry and Seafood

- Beef
- Bork
- Poultry (chicken, duck, etc)
- Lamb
- Seafood
- Lobster
- Shrimp
- scallops

Vegetables

- Carrots
- Broccoli
- Cauliflower
- Pepper
- Asparagus
- Potatoes (baby reds or golden yellow)
- Mushrooms
- Onions
- Celery

Fruits

- Apples
- Bananas
- Strawberries
- Oranges
- Pears
- pineaple

Breads

- Sour dough
- French or Italian
- Focaccia

Desserts

- Rice Krispie treats
- Angel food cake
- Pound cake
- Small cookies such has lady fingers
- Cheesecake
- Marshmallows
- Brownies

FONDUE QUICK TIPS

Step #1: Determine how much food is needed

- A person can eat about 20 one-inches cubes of bread (1/2 to 1/3 of a loaf of French bread), 8 ounces of meat, 6 ounces of fish or seafood, four to six ounces of cheese, six to eight ounces of vegetables, six to eight ounces of fruit, four cookies and two to three ounces of a dessert sauce.
- Determine the food types (i.e., cheese, main entrée, or dessert) and ration out how much on average each person would eat.
- Typically, a total of one pound of food per person.

Step #2: Size and preparation of the food

- Cut all ingredients for dipping into one or two bite sizes or one inch cubes
- Prepare raw meat by removing fat and marinating (optional).
- Prepare seafood by washing and cutting into bite size pieces. Shrimp should be deveined.
- Prepare vegetables by trimming, washing and cutting into bite size pieces. Blanch or lightly steam vegetables to make them tender. Potatoes can be boiled in advance and then will brown nicely in the oil.
- Lemon juice is recommended to minimize browning on vegetables.
- Arrange the different types of raw meat together to avoid cross contamination. Store in the refrigerator until ready to begin. Raw meats and seafood should not be left at room temperature for more than two hours.
- Meat and vegetables should be dry before emersing in hot oil or broth to prevent dangerous splatters.

Step #3: Choosing the right type of fondue pot

- Ceramic pots are best used for cheese, chocolate and other dessert fondues that are "dips" that do not require high heat.
- Electric metal pots are best used with broth, oil, wine or beer fondue recipes in which the food is cooked in the pot such as meat or seafood. These pots can be used for cheese fondues as long as the heat is kept at a lower temperature.

Step #4: Choosing the right type of fondue: oil or broth to cook, or cheese or chocolate to dip

- Use flavorful liquids. Use a wine or beer that you would prefer drinking. If you wouldn't drink it, don't cook with it.
- For oil fondues, use a flavorless vegetable or peanut oil. Season meats that are cooked in oil after. This will prevent overcooked seasonings and impacted others meals.
- Tempura or a beer batter can be used in an oil base fondue on meats, seafoods, poultry and vegetables. Be sure to keep meat, seafood and vegetable batters separate from one another to avoid cross contamination.

Step #5: Preheating your sauce before transferring to the fondue pot

- Preheat the oil, broth or wine to 375° F (just below boiling) on the stove or in the fondue pot.
- Do not transfer hot oil from a separate pan into a fondue pot.
- To prevent the oil from spattering or bubbling over, do not fill the pot more than one-third full.

Step #6: Choosing the correct cheese type

- Rubbing a clove of garlic to the bottom of a fondue pot before adding the cheese will enhance its flavor.
- Adding alcohol such as wine, champagne or beer not only adds flavor but helps prevent the cheese from curdling.
- A Sauvignon Blanc, Pinot Grigio, Champagne or Presecco works well with a cheese fondue. Chardonnays and red wines are not recommended. Red wines lack color appeal. The taste of a chardonnay can be overwhelming in a cheese fondue.
- Shredded cheese melts more easily. Do not allow the cheese to boil. It may seize.
- If the cheese fondue starts to curdle, mix in some freshly squeezed lemon juice. Stir constantly with a wooden spoon until the fondue is smooth.
- To adjust the thickness, add wine or apple cider (not water)

Step #7: Choosing the correct broth

- Use a homemade stock that has been strained or a purchased low sodium stock that is flavorful. High sodium stock will become more concentrated as it is cooked.
- Season broths with fresh ginger, green onions, spices or fresh herbs for flavorful dipping.
- Have additional hot stock or broth available to add to the fondue pot as necessary.

Step #8: Choosing the right chocolate or dessert fondue

- Be sure to use the best chocolate available for the optimum flavor.
- Finely chop the chocolate into 1 inch or smaller pieces.
- Do not allow chocolate to boil or it may sieze.

Step #9: Fondue etiquette

- Food should not be eaten from the fondue fork but transferred first to the individual plates and/or fork.
- No double dipping by placing partially eaten foods back into the fondue pot, regardless of how hot the oil or broth may be. It's still germ sharing.

Step #10: Suggested fondue accessories and serving pieces

- Long fondue forks, preferably color coded to know who the "owner" is.
- Individual plates for cooked and uncooked foods. Never mix uncooked with cooked foods. Compartmentalized plates work best.
- Dinner forks that are used for eating the food only. The fondue fork is for cooking, not eating to minimize cross contamination.
- Plenty of napkins.
- Dipping sauces or spices are optional but very tasty and add to the experience.

Step #11: Seasonings for dipped fondues

- Based upon personal preference one can use additional seasonings and dips that shouldn't be cooked to enhance flavors such as garlic salts, teriyaki sauce, etc.

STEAK FONDUE

- ½ C Butter
- 24 oz. Peanut oil

Cook oil and butter on medium high heat. Serve with sirloin or filet mignon based upon personal preference.

- 6 oz Medium sharp cheddar cheese
- 2 oz Emmenthaler Swiss Cheese
- 4 oz Beer (can be non-alcoholic)
- 2 t Chopped garlic
- 2 t Worcestershire sauce
- 2 t Flour
- 2 t Dry mustard powder

CHEDDAR CHEESE FONDUE

Serves: 4

If you are using a fondue pot turn it onto medium heat, otherwise, use a double boiler to heat this mixture in. Place beer, garlic, mustard powder, and Worcestershire sauce, and combine well. Shred or cube all cheese, and toss with flour, coating cheese well. The flour will help thicken the sauce. When the beer mixture is warm add one third of the cheese into the mixture, and whisk very well. Once the cheese has been incorporated well, add second third of cheese, whisk in very well, and add in the remaining cheese and whisk until nice and smooth.

Can use non-alcholic beer if prefer! Beer taste makes the taste very flavorful.

CLASSIC CHEESE FONDUE

- 1 clove Garlic
- 1 cup Dy white wine
- 10 oz. Emmentaler cheese, diced or shredded
- 10 oz. Gruyere cheese, diced or shredded
- 1 ½ T Potato flour or Cornstarch
- ¼ t Ground white pepper
- pinch of freshly grated nutmeg
- crusty bread, cut into cubes for serving

Rub a medium, heavy saucepan with garlic. Discard garlic pieces or finely chop and add them to saucepan. Place pot over medium-high heat, add wine and bring just to a boil. Immediately reduce heat to low and add cheese. It should melt very slowly, be sure to stir slowly in a figure-8 pattern until all cheese is melted (approximately 5 minutes). If it melts too fast it will become tough and stringy. Add potato flour or cornstarch, pepper, and nutmeg. Simmer for about 2 minutes. Do not let it boil, sputtering is ok. It will thicken when it is brought to the table. Pour the fondue into a warmed pot and serve immediately.

THREE CHEESE FONDUE

- 1 C White wine
- 1 T Butter
- 1 T All-purpose flour
- 7 oz Gruyere cheese, shredded or cubed
- 7 oz Sharp cheddar cheese, shredded
- 7 oz Emmentaler cheese, shredded or cubed.

1. Bring the wine to a boil in a small saucepan. Melt the butter in a medium saucepan over medium low heat. Whisk in the flour and cook for about 5 minutes, stirring constantly to avoid sticking and burning.

2. Once the flour mixture is heated thoroughly, stir the wine into the flour mixture slowly. Use a whisk to smooth the mixture. Slowly add cubes or the shredded Gruyere, cheddar and Emmentaler cheese. Stir until cheese is melted. Transfer cheese mixture to fondue pot. Keep warm over low flame.

PESTO CHEESE FONUDE

- 1 lb Part-skim mozzarella cheese, shredded
- 8 oz Italian Fontina cheese, shredded
- 6 oz Provolone, shredded
- 2 T Cornstarch
- 1 T Extra virgin olive oil
- 1 oz Shallot, peeled and chopped
- 1 clove Garlic, peeled and chopped
- 2 C Dry white wine
- 6 T Pesto

1. Place cheeses in a large bowl and sprinkle with cornstarch. Toss gently to completely coat. Set aside.

2. Heat the olive oil in the fondue pot. Cook the chopped shallot and garlic until tender and golden, about one minute on medium heat. Add the wine and bring to a simmer. Reduce temperature to medium low to medium (simmer). Gradually add the cheese, one handful at a time. Stir or mix in and add more cheese until all is melted. Once all of the cheese is melted, stir in the pesto.

CRAB AND CHEDDAR FONDUE

- ¾ C Dry cider or beer
- 1 T Fresh lemon juice
- pinch Sugar
- 1 lb. Sharp cheddar cheese, shredded
- 2 T All-purpose flour
- 7 oz. Fresh lump crabmeat, picked over for shells
- 1 t caraway seed, lightly toasted
- ½ t salt, or to taste
- pinch Cayenne pepper
- cubes of crusty bread for serving

In a double boiler over simmering water, heat the beer or cider, sugar and lemon juice. Combine cheese with flour in a separate bowl. When liquid is hot, reduce heat, slowly let it melt (about 5 minutes). Heat crab in microwave on medium high until warm (about 30 seconds). This will help prevent the cheese from curdling. Add crabmeat, salt, caraway seed, and cayenne to the melted cheese. Transfer to fondue pot and serve with crusty bread.

CHEDDAR, ONION, APPLE AND CIDER FONDUE

- 1 ½ lb Extra sharp cheddar cheese, shredded
- 2 ½ T Cornstarch
- ½ t Dry mustard
- 1 T Unsalted butter
- 1 oz Shallot, peeled and chopped
- ½ C Tart apple, finely diced
- 2 ½ C Hard cider

Place cheese in a large bowl and sprinkle with cornstarch and dry mustard. Toss gently to completely coat. Set aside. Heat the butter in the fondue pot on medium heat. Cook the shallot and apple in the butter until tender and golden for about three to four minutes. Add 2 cups of the cider and bring to a boil. Reduce the heat to medium and gradually add the cheese, one handful at a time until well mixed and melted. Use extra cider to thin as needed.

BEEF BROTH FONDUE

- 6 C Beef stock or low sodium broth
- 3 Scallions, cut in 1 inch pieces
- 6 slices Fresh ginger, finely sliced
- 1 – 2 Cloves of garlic, peeled and halved
- 4 Peppercorns, whole
- 1 T Soy sauce
- 1 T Rice wine or dry sherry

Mix the beef stock/broth, scallions, ginger, garlic and peppercorns in fondue pot. Bring to a boil. Reduce to medium and simmer for 20 – 25 minutes to allow the broth to absorb the flavors of the ginger and scallions.

Suggested: thinly sliced beef, pork, crisp tender carrots, mushrooms.

SEAFOOD BOUILLABAISSE FONDUE

- 1 T Extra Virgin Oil
- 3 cloves Garlic, peeled and sliced thinly
- 1 lb fresh mussels, cleaned and bearded
- 1 pinch Saffron threads
- 2 C Dry white wine
- 1 t Kosher salt
- 26 oz Tomato sauce or puree
- 3-4 Sprigs of fresh basil
- 1 C Water
- 1 lb Large shrimp
- 1 lb Sea scallops

Heat oil on medium high. Add the garlic and cook until lightly browned, approximately one minute. Add mussels (in shell), saffron and wine to pot. Stirring occasionally, cook until mussels are opened, approximately three to four minutes. Remove mussels from the pot. Add salt, tomato sauce/puree, basil and water to pot. Increase the temperature to high and bring to a boil. Reduce temperature to medium and simmer for ten minutes. Remove mussels from their shells and discard shells.

Remove the basil sprigs. If sauce is too thin, thin with a little water. To serve, skewer the shrimp, scallops or mussels onto fondue forks and dip into the sauce. Cook shrimp and scallops until firm but not tough.   Cook mussels just to heat through. Crusty French bread is also ideal for dipping.

ROCKY ROAD FONDUE

- *10 oz Milk chocolate, chopped*
- *½ C Sweetened condensed milk*
- *½ C Heavy cream*
- *1 T Espresso or strong coffee*
- *1 T Rum (optional)*
- *4 oz Small marshmallows*
- *½ C Mixture of unsalted and toasted hazelnut, pecans, and walnuts*

For dipping

- *8 Lady finger biscotti or lady fingers*
- *4 oz Large Marshmallows*
- *Pint of Fresh Strawberries*

Heat milk chocolate, milk, cream, and espresso in double boiler. Stir gently until mixture is melted. Transfer to fondue pot and slowly stir in the small marshmallows. Use large marshmallows, fruit, and biscotte or lady fingers to dip into fondue.

CHOCOLATE HAZELNUT FONDUE

- 1 ½ C Half and half
- 1 C Heavy cream
- 1 ½ lbs Semi-sweet chocolate, finely chopped
- ¼ C Frangelico liqueur
- ¼ C Toasted hazelnuts
- ¼ C Chopped toasted hazelnuts

Place the half and half and heavy cream in the fondue pot. Heat creams on medium until the cream is bubbling. Reduce the heat to medium and gradually stir in the chocolate, a handful at a time and continue stirring until melted. Add the liqueur. Keep warm on medium low. Sprinkle with chopped hazelnuts just before serving.

WARM BERRY FONDUE

- 5 – 6 C Mixed fresh or frozen berries (such as blackberries, strawberries, blueberries, raspberries)
- ½ C Sparkling wine
- 4 T Cornstarch mixed with 2 tablespoons of water; stir until smooth
- 1/3 C Fruit or nut flavored liqueur

Puree the berries (except ½ cup). Using a fine mesh sieve or cheese cloth with funnel, press out the liquid. The seeds should be discarded.

Cook the remaining puree without the seeds on medium heat (stove top). Stir frequently until bubbling gently; cook for 4 – 5 minutes. Stir in the cornstarch mixture and cook until it thickens. Transfer to the fondue pot and stir in the liqueur and keep warm.

CLASSIC CHOCOLATE FONDUE

- 1 C   Whipping cream
- 8 oz Premium chocolate, chopped
- 2 t   Orange liqueur (such as Grand Marnier)
- Various sliced fruits and/or dessert treats, for dipping

Over low flame, heat cream until warm, but do not bring to a boil. Pour in chocolate while stirring continuously. Mixture will become smooth. Stir in liqueur and transfer to a fondue pot.

DIPPING SAUCES FOR MEAT, POULTRY OR SEAFOOD FONDUES

MUSHROOM SAUCE:

- *2 T   Sherry*
- *½ can Beef gravy*
- *1 t   Grated onion*
- *3 lg. Mushrooms, chopped*

For each sauce, mix all ingredients in a small bowl to serve.

MUSTARD SAUCE:

- *¾ C Mayonnaise*
- *2 T   Wine vinegar*
- *1 T   Dry mustard*
- *3 T   Hot mustard*

Other store bought sauces that are quick and easy and make the meal complete include:
A1-Steak sauce - Ranch Dressing – Ketchup - Blue Cheese dressing - Soy Sauce – Barbeque sauce.

A LADIES LUNCH - NANETTE KELLEY AND MARY PACCHINI

WINTER WHITE SANGRIA

- *1 bottle of chilled white wine*
- *¼ cup of brandy*
- *¼ cups sugar*
- *2 cups of club soda*
- *1 whole lemon sliced*
- *1 whole lime sliced*
- *1 whole granny smith apple sliced*
- *1 bunch of red grapes*

Mix first 4 ingredients in a tall glass pitcher of punch bowl, add 2-3 cups of ice. Add all of the fruit slices and enjoy!

CHINESE CHICKEN SALAD

Chicken:

- 1 lb. of bones skinned chicken breast (approximately 4 chicken halves)
- Bottled oriental marinade of combination of Italian dressing/soy teriyaki

Salad:

- 1 lb finely shredded cabbage
- 6 green onions, chopped
- 2 pkg. Raman noodle soup mix (Chicken or Oriental)
- ¼ cup of slivered almonds
- 4-5 T. of sesame seeds

Salad Dressing:

- 5 T. red wine vinegar
- ¾ cup salad oil
- 3 T. sugar
- ½ t. black pepper
- 2 drops of sesame oil
- 2 flavor packets of Ramen Noodle Soup

1. Marinade chicken for 1-2 hours, then grill on stove (using grill pan) or on outside grill or bake in the oven at 350 degrees until done. Cut chicken in thin slices to lay over top of salad

2 Brown seeds and almonds for 5 minutes @ 300 degrees. Crush noodles and combine with cabbage, onion, sesame seeds and almonds.

3. Mix and shake well all dressing ingredients and, combine with salad right before serving. Plate the salad, then top with sliced grilled chicken.

BASIL BISCUITS:

- 1 pkg. of Pillsbury Grand Biscuits
- ½ stick butter – melted
- 2 T. grated parmesan cheese
- ½ t. basil
- garlic to taste

You will need a 9" round cake pan to begin

1. On the bottom of the pan, pour melted butter, sprinkle cheese and basil. Add garlic to taste. Cut biscuits into quarters. Place into pan as a whole biscuit, any remaining space along the sides, cut biscuit dough smaller to fit.

2. Bake at 350 degrees for 20-25 minutes until golden brown.

SWEDISH CREAM DESSERT

- *1 pint of whipping cream*
- *1 cup of sugar*
- *1 envelope Knox unflavored gelatin*
- *1 pint of sour cream*
- *1 tsp. vanilla*
- *Fresh fruit – raspberries, blueberries or sliced strawberries make a nice presentation when completed in tall champagne glasses*

Mix whipping cream, sugar, and gelatin and stir over low heat until sugar dissolves. Cool 5 minutes and add sour cream and vanilla. Add 1-2 tablespoons of cream to champagne glass, layer with fruit, and another layer of cream and top with a layer of fruit.

SUPER EASY RECIPES- SHARON
TAYLOR AND LYN CROSBY

SUPER EASY CARROT SOUFFLE'

- 2 cans carrots, drained
- ½ cup melted butter or margarine
- 3 eggs
- ½ cup sugar
- 4 T. flour
- 1 tsp. vanilla
- 1 tsp baking powder
- Cinnamon to taste
- Brown sugar

Mix with electric mixer all the ingredients together except brown sugar. Pour into greased pan. Sprinkle top with brown sugar. Bake at 350 degrees for 45 minutes.

SUPER EASY BAKED BRIE CHEESE

- ½ lb. Brie Cheese with skin on
- 1 small can crushed pineapple
- 1 small package slivered almonds

Spray microwave-safe baking dish with non-stick spray. Place Brie in dish and pour crushed pineapple over cheese. Sprinkle top with slivered almonds. Cover dish with lid or plastic wrap and microwave until cheese is fully melted. Serve with cocktail bread or crackers.

EASY SHRIMP AND BROCCOLI

Serves 4

- *2 tablespoons olive oil*
- *1 – 2 cloves of garlic cut in chunks*
- *1 pound frozen shrimp deveined and tail off*
- *1 head broccoli crowns – cleaned and cut*
- *1 can low sodium chicken broth*
- *½ cup chopped onion*
- *½ cup Parmesan cheese*

Cook in a covered frying/sauté pan

1. Begin by placing the garlic chunks and olive oil in the pan. Turn the flame to low and let the garlic simmer for about 10 – 15 minutes. Remove the garlic chunks.

2. Sauté the onion in the olive oil until clear.

3. Toss the broccoli in the olive oil and onion and sauté until bright green.

4. Add the frozen shrimp and toss to coat.

5. Add can of chicken broth and Parmesan cheese, stir.

6. Cover and simmer for 15 – 20 minutes.

Can serve over pasta or rice or with roasted potatoes.

ROASTED PURPLE PERUVIAN POTATOES

Oven 400º

Buy enough potatoes to feed your family. These potatoes are bite size. Approximately ½ cup of largely diced onions

To Roast:

1. Thoroughly wash potatoes. Pat dry. Cut in half and toss with olive oil and onions to lightly coat.

2. Spread in single layer on prepared cookie sheet – cut side up – roast on center rack of oven for 20 minutes. Flip potatoes and sprinkle with Parmesan cheese to taste. Continue cooking for approximately 15 minutes.

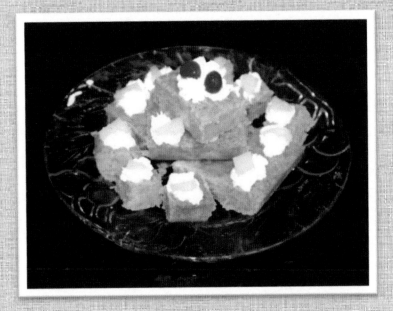

SUPER EASY PINEAPPLE DESSERT

- 4 c. bread crumbs
- 1 c. melted butter
- 1 (20 oz.) can crushed or chunk pineapple
- 2 c. sugar
- 3 beaten eggs
- 1 c. milk

Combine bread crumbs, sugar, butter and eggs. Add pineapple and milk. Pour in greased 9 x 13 inch dish. Bake 45-50 minutes at 325 degrees

THANKSGIVING SIDES –MARIETTE KAPLAN AND FAMILY

Thanksgiving dinner for a crowd is easy when the kids pitch in. They all make their special side dish which has become a great family tradition. The dishes can be prepared a day in advance. I take them out of the refrigerator an hour or so before cooking. When the turkey comes out of the oven to rest, I throw the sides in. Thirty minutes later the turkey is ready to be carved and the sides are done. I believe that there is no easier dinner to prepare that receives as many compliments as the traditional Thanksgiving feast. When everyone helps out it makes a heartwarming tradition which memories last a lifetime.

BRYCE'S PUMPKIN MUFFINS

- 3 cups sugar
- 1 cup oil
- 4 eggs beaten
- 2/3 cup water
- 2 cups of canned pumpkin
- 1 1/2 t. salt
- 1 t. cinnamon
- 1 t. nutmeg
- 3 1/3 cups sifted flour
- 2 t. baking soda

1. Preheat oven to 325

2. Mix together: sugar, oil, eggs. Water and canned pumpkin

3. Sift together and add to mixture salt, cinnamon, nutmeg, flour and baking soda

4. Pour into greased mini muffin pans- makes about 36 mini muffins

5. Bake at 325 for 18 minutes

MORGAN'S MASHED POTATO BAKE

Serves 8 to 10.

- *1 pound Yukon Gold potatoes*
- *1/2 cup butter*
- *1/2 cup parmesan cheese*
- *4 cloves minced garlic*
- *salt and pepper*

Cook potatoes in a pot of salted water until tender but still firm.

Drain and return to pot.

Add butter, parmesan cheese, cream cheese, garlic, salt and pepper

Use potato masher or mixer until smooth.

Can serve immediately or can put into a casserole dish and bake at 350 for 30 minutes.

CHELSEA'S SWEET POTATO SOUFFLE

Serves 10

Souffle

- 3 cups cooked mashed sweet potatoes or yams
- 1 cup sugar
- 1/2 t. salt
- 2 eggs
- 2 1/2 T of melted butter or margarine
- 1/2 cup of milk
- 1 t. vanilla extract

Crunch topping - mix together

- 4 T butter or margarine melted
- 1 cup brown sugar
- 1/3 cup flour
- 1 cup chopped pecans

1. Mix all Souffle ingredients. Pour into greased baking dish. Cover with crunch topping.

2. Sprinkle pecans over top

3. Bake at 350 for 30 minutes

GARRETT'S GREEN BEAN CASSEROLE

12 servings

- *3 T butter*
- *1 cup chopped onion*
- *1 bag 32 oz. green beans or 8 cups fresh cooked green beans.*
- *2-10.75 oz. cans of cream of mushroom or potato or celery soup*
- *1/2 cup of milk*
- *3 T soy sauce*
- *1/4 t. black pepper*
- *2 2/3 cup French's French Fried Onions*
- *2 cups shredded cheddar cheese*

1. Warm frozen green beans in casserole dish in microwave.

2. Melt butter in large skillet. Stir in onions and saute until transparent.

3. Add soup, milk, soy sauce, salt and pepper and stir.

4. Transfer to casserole dish with green beans and stir in 2 cups french fried onions.

5. Top with shredded cheddar cheese

6. Bake at 350 for 30 minutes and stir.

7. Top with remaining onions and serve.

ALL CREPES - TERESA ABASCAL

Making crepes is a fun experience, and can be a rewarding one. In France, specifically, they are very popular and you can eat them at street corners, filled with sweet and savory delicious and endless fillings. I like to prepare the crepes in advance while spending time with my family, and then have a day or two to come up with ideas for the fillings we can all indulge in.

I love the versatility of this dish. It can be served individually for a romantic dinner, for a small group of friends, or it can be served family style in large trays, from which a larger group can help themselves. I have even prepared large quantities for parties of 40 people. Everyone loves them! They can be rolled like tacos, or they can be folded in small square or triangular pockets.

Here, I am giving the recipes for a breakfast crepe, a vegetarian option, and a couple of sweet crepe delights; the popular nutella crepe, and a dulce de leche option.

You can buy the crepes or make them yourself. The good part of making them is that you can try new colors (with some herbs, blended with the batter, new flavors, sizes, or even thickness although they should be as thin as possible.)

CREPES

(approximately 30 crepes)

- *2 cups flour*
- *4 eggs*
- *2 cups milk*
- *2 cups sparkling water*
- *½ teaspoon salt*
- *2 sticks melted butter*

1. Add all ingredients in the blender until a smooth consistency batter forms. Let it sit in the fridge for an hour. If consistency is too runny, add a tablespoon of flour. If it is thick, add milk.

If you don't have the special crepe maker, use a 8" non-stick fry pan.

2. Heat the pan in medium heat. If it is too hot, the crepes will burn and become hard to fold or roll.

3. Pour enough batter to cover the pan and quickly swirl it to cover all the surface. Make this as thin as possible, but cover any holes that may form with a little more batter. Let it sit for some seconds and when you can loosen it with a spatula, flip it over. It will cook very fast. Remove the crepe and slide it into a plate. Stack the crepes and let them cool if you are not using them immediately. If used one or two days after, make sure you warm them up for a little bit in the microwave oven, so they do not stick and break when you try to separate them.

BREAKFAST CREPES

- 5 slices of bacon
- 6 eggs
- ¾ cup grated cheddar cheese
- salt and pepper
- ½ cup maple syrup
- Cilantro or parsley leaves for decoration

1. Cook the bacon with its own fat until crispy. Remove excess fat with paper towels.

2. Scramble the eggs with salt and pepper to taste.

3. When eggs are done, add the cheese.

4. Add some of the egg mixture to each crepe and roll as a taco.

5. Sprinkle the bacon on top and drizzle with maple syrup.

6. Decorate with some parsley or cilantro leaves.

VEGETARIAN CREPES

- *2 Tbs vegetable oil*
- *3 chopped scallions*
- *½ cup chopped leek*
- *1 poblano pepper seeded and chopped in small squares*
- *1 chopped or grated carrot*
- *2 finely diced zucchinis*
- *¾ cup corn kernels*
- *1 shedded tomato (this eliminates the skin, but leaves all the flesh which gives consistency to the whole dish)*
- *1 packet liquid vegetable flavor boost (optional)*
- *salt and pepper*
- *10 oz feta cheese*

Bechamel Sauce

- *1 cup melting cheese grated*
- *For the Bechamel Sauce*
- *4 Tbs butter*
- *½ onion diced*
- *5 Tbs Flour*
- *2 cups milk*
- *Dash of nutmeg*
- *Salt and Pepper*

1. Heat the oil in a cooking pan, add the scallions and leek and cook until they are transparent and start releasing their fragrance.

2. Add the poblano and cook until they are a little soft.

3. Add the carrots and let them cook for a couple of minutes and add the zucchinis.

4. After two more minutes add the corn and the tomato.

5. Add the vegetable boost, salt and pepper to taste.
Cook until all flavors blend. Remove from the stove and let it cool.

6. Fill the crepes with the vegetables and add about a teaspoon feta cheese on each one. Roll like tacos. Pour the bechamel sauce and sprinkle the cheese on top.
Bake in the oven just until the cheese starts turning gold.

Bechamel Sauce

1. Heat the butter and the onion in low heat until the onion is cooked and transparent. Add the flour and keep moving until a thick paste forms and it is slightly brown. Start adding the milk little by little or the flour paste won't dissolve. Whisk and season with nutmeg, salt and pepper.

2. Continue whisking until it is thick and cooked. Remove from the heat.

NUTELLA CREPES

- Nutella
- Fruit such as bananas or strawberries
- Chocolate syrup
- Powdered sugar

Fill each crepe with Nutella and some fruit and fold in triangles, like a napkin.

Drizzle with chocolate syrup and powdered sugar

DULCE DE LECHE CREPES

- *1 cup of Dulce de leche or Mexican Cajeta*
- *2 Tbs favorite liquor such as Kalua or frangelico or rum to thin the dulce de leche*
- *½ cup finely chopped pecans or walnuts*
- *vainilla ice cream*

1. Warm the dulce the leche and liquor to thin it.

2. Fill each crepe with a spoonful of warm "*dulce de leche*" and fold in squares.

3. Pour another spoonful of dulce de leche and some nuts on top.

4. Place a scoop of ice cream on top.

Serve warm.

TRADITIONAL JEWISH DINNERS
- LAUREN MARGOLIN

Family traditions are part of what makes coming together for the holidays fun and memorable. Whether it's the smell of a roasted turkey, the mess in the kitchen, the many hands helping, the setting of the table or the reunion of your family; holidays, especially the Jewish ones, are something I hope will stay in my children's minds and hearts so that they will carry on and continue with some of the most fabulous recipes.

For the record, I'm what my dad calls a 'pedestrian' eater. I'm not that brave in trying new things and I've become allergic to a ton of different foods as I get older. Because I love to cook however, I work hard to tweak and create recipes that are easy to make, often able to prepare ahead of time and most importantly, that taste good! Some of the recipes I'll be sharing in my chapter, Jew Food, have come down from my mother, both my maternal and paternal grandmas and my mother-in-law and you'll note that some recipes, like my mother-in-law's Jello mold, isn't necessarily traditional Jew Food, but it's expected at every Jewish holiday just because it tastes good.

Because many of these recipes can be used at any of the Jewish holidays or Shabbat dinners on Friday nights, I'm going to group them into two completely delicious Jewish inspired meals. A fresh Challah is welcome with both of these selections.

NOTES:

- *I do not keep Kosher. I'm sure you can adapt any of these meals to be Kosher if you wish.*
- *Some of these recipes can be adapted for Passover by substituting cake meal for the flour.*
- *There are many other traditional Jewish foods that are not represented: Noodle Kugel, Matzo Ball soup, Kreplach (dumplings), Stuffed Cabbage, Challah and Charoset (apples, nuts and wine). These are all delicious foods and I can see my sister rolling her eyes for not including them, but alas, the foods I have chosen are just that, my choice. Also, I'm a firm believer in the Manachevitz packaged mix for Matzo Ball Soup and no one bakes a better Challah than a baker!*

COMPLETE DINNER #1

Brisket - Carrot Soufflé - Roasted Asparagus - Slow Roasted Potatoes – Strawberry Jello Mold

BRISKET

This is a simple recipe with excellent results. If you've never bought a brisket before, here's the scoop. First, make sure it's a first cut piece of meat. Have the butcher trim it up for you. Fat is good, but not too much. A thin layer on one side is best. Also, ask them to score both sides for you so you slice it correctly. This is a cut of meat that you must slice against the grain! Brisket is best when made ahead so that the rendered gravy further tenderizes the meat while refrigerated overnight or frozen. Although Jews have been eating brisket since forever, it is also a very popular cut of meat in the south for barbequing because it takes a long time to cook or smoke. Brisket is also the cut of meat used for corned beef and pastrami.

- 4 -5 lb. first cut brisket
- 1 can whole berry cranberry sauce
- 1 can water
- 2 packets Lipton onion soup mix
- 1 small jar Ragu tomato sauce

1. Rinse brisket and put in large roasting pan with the fat side UP. There is a huge debate on this subject for brisket makers, but really, the answer is clear. The fat juices should drip down into the meat!

2. In separate bowl, mix together sauce ingredients. Pour sauce over brisket and make sure the sauce gets under it as well. With heavy-duty tin foil, cover brisket with a slight tent, but secure edges well. Cook in a preheated 350-degree oven for 3 ½ hours. When cool, remove from pan and slice on a diagonal against the grain! Arrange in pan and pour gravy all over. Refrigerate if serving next day or freeze up to 3 months. When ready to serve, reheat in 350-degree oven until it's completely heated through. If it starts to brown on top, cover with foil while in oven.

CARROT SOUFFLÉ

This is a flat out winner whenever I make it and has not only become a Jewish holiday tradition but also a Thanksgiving one. It's easy and you can make the day before! Note: unless I'm making this just for my family of 4, you must double this.

- 1 lb. can cut or sliced carrots
- 3 eggs
- 3 Tbs. flour
- ½ cup sugar
- 1 tsp. vanilla
- 1 stick melted margarine
- dash nutmeg
- dash cinnamon

Topping:

- 1/3-cup corn flake crumbs
- 3 Tbs. brown sugar
- 2 Tbs. melted margarine

1. Drain carrots from can then puree carrots and eggs in blender or Cuisinart. Once pureed, add the rest of the ingredients to the mixture. Blend well. Pour into a 1-½ qt. casserole that has been well greased. (If doubling recipe, use 9x13.) Crumble topping across top of carrot mixture.

2. Bake in a 350-degree oven for 50 minutes. If making the day before, cook for about 30 minutes and then refrigerate once it's come to down to room temperature. Bake for an additional 30 minutes before serving. Pre-cut in squares while in pan so it's easier to get out.

ROASTED ASPARAGUS

- *1 or 2 bunches of fresh, thin asparagus. (They should be tender and green in color)*
- *Olive oil*
- *Kosher salt*
- *Pepper*

I'm a firm believer that any vegetable from Brussels sprout to cauliflower is best when roasted. Simple to do and again, you can make the day before. Remember, veggies shrink when cooked so eyeball it correctly. Consider 5 asparagus per person.

Gently snap off each rough end of the asparagus at its natural breaking point. Rinse under cool water and dry thoroughly. On a cookie/baking sheet with sides or a tinfoil cookie sheet, line up asparagus with as little overlap as possible. Drizzle some good, light tasting extra virgin olive oil on top and then with your hands, roll the asparagus so that all sides are covered. (This is great for getting soft hands!) Generously sprinkle with kosher salt and some pepper. If making day ahead, cover now and refrigerate. When ready to serve, bake in a 350-degree oven for about 20-25 minutes. Can serve as is, or grate some fresh Parmesan cheese on top.

SLOW ROASTED POTATOES

You can never go wrong with a potato that has been slow roasted. This recipe is similar to the asparagus but potatoes take much longer to roast and I usually add onions to the potatoes. These onions caramelize beautifully and it's a great introduction for kids to onions. There is no Judaic significance for potatoes, however many people relate potato latkes with Chanukah. That is true, we eat potato latkes at Chanukah, but only because they are fried in oil, which symbolizes the oil lamp that only had oil for a day and miraculously lasted 8 days and 8 nights in the Jews fight for freedom.

- *1 stick melted margarine*
- *1 c. canola oil*
- *1 bag mini red-skinned potatoes*
- *1 bag mini yellow-skinned potatoes*
- *3-5 red onions sliced in thin rings*
- *parsley (dried is fine)*
- *kosher salt*
- *garlic powder*
- *paprika*

Wash but do not peel the potatoes. Dry well. Cut into quarters or halves but try and keep size of all potatoes consistent. Put in large roasting pan with onions. Pour melted margarine, then the oil all over potatoes; gently mix well so that all potatoes and onions are coated. Season liberally with parsley flakes, salt, garlic powder and paprika. Paprika is important because it helps with the browning process. Bake in a 375-degree oven for 1-2 hours, until potatoes are browned nicely. Toss occasionally while cooking.

STRAWBERRY JELLO MOLD

- 3 (3-oz.) pkgs. strawberry Jello
- 3 c. boiling water
- 2 c. of drained juice from the frozen strawberries
- 2 (16-oz.) pkg. frozen strawberries, thawed and drained (RESERVE the juice from draining)
- 1 (9-oz.) Cool Whip

Until moving to the Midwest, I had never had a Jello mold. They have now become a staple on holidays and the most famous one is this.

Dissolve Jello in boiling water. Add cold water. Chill until thickened. Once completely chilled whip the Jello with mixer then add the Cool Whip and beat until well blended. Gently fold in strawberries. Put in a well-sprayed (with original Pam) mold pan until set, usually overnight. Invert on plate and serve. Garnish with whole berries. Note: you may need to run some hot water on sides of mold to help loosen it from mold pan.

COMPLETE DINNER #2

Roasted Turkey with Matzo Stuffing - Candied Sweet Potatoes - Seal and Soak Veggies - Honey Cake

ROASTED TURKEY WITH MATZO STUFFING:

- *20 lb. turkey*
- *6 eggs*
- *Several onions*
- *Peanut oil*
- *Vegetable oil*
- *Stick of butter*
- *Chopped garlic*
- *Carrots*
- *Celery stalks*
- *Matzo*
- *Salt*
- *Pepper*
- *Paprika*
- *Garlic Powder*
- *Onion Powder*
- *String and strong, large-eyed needle to sew turkey shut*

This is a no fail whole turkey recipe. Certainly the same idea can be done on a turkey breast if you only want white meat. I am sharing this recipe exactly as my mom transcribed it to me. If you haven't made a whole turkey you'll love this because my mom knows I love step-by-step instructions. Her matzo stuffing is famous and it's welcome not just on Passover, but on all holidays.

1. For about a 20 pound turkey, sauté 3 medium chopped onions in peanut oil for a few minutes. Add 2 - 3 smashed and chopped garlic cloves. In Cuisinart, chop 3 stalks celery and 3 carrots (or 3 handfuls of baby carrots chopped) and add to sauté pan. Season with salt and pepper. Add more peanut oil if pan looks too dry and sauté for about 25 minutes until veggies soften and come together. (Note: you can do this the day before -- just let veggies cool, then put in covered dish and refrigerate.)

2. After you have cleaned and dried the turkey thoroughly, you can start putting the stuffing together. Put 6 large eggs and about 1/4-cup water in large bowl. Beat well. Add a little salt and pepper to egg and water mixture. Take about 9 pieces of plain matzo. In batches of 3 pieces, run them under water, and break into pieces and add to egg mixture. I add a little more salt and pepper now, too. Combine and then mix into the onion mixture until well blended.

3. You are ready to stuff turkey. Turkey will have put out more liquid, so blot body, neck and chest cavities again. Season the two cavities with salt, pepper, garlic and onion powders. Stuff the neck first, and sew closed with heavy thread. Put turkey in roasting pan and then stuff chest cavity and sew closed. Tuck wing tips under body and tie legs together. Make a seasoning rub of salt, pepper, garlic powder, onion powder, and paprika. Rub entire turkey with vegetable oil, and then seasoning rub. Cut up pieces of butter and put all over turkey. Put quartered onion pieces, baby carrots, and celery pieces around turkey. Tent pan with aluminum foil and roast at 350 degrees. After about one hour, add a little chicken broth to enhance pan drippings, and baste turkey. Continue to roast and baste every hour until meat thermometer reads 180 degrees at thick part of thigh (or if your turkey has pop-up device -- when it pops up).

VERY IMPORTANT -- ONCE TURKEY IS STUFFED, ROAST AT ONCE. YOU CANNOT LEAVE A STUFFED BIRD SITTING, so judge your time wisely.

When turkey is done, let it rest for about 20 minutes before carving.

CANDIED SWEET POTATOES

- *6 medium sweet potatoes*
- *Peanut oil*
- *Sugar*

Rinse (no need to scrub) potatoes to remove surface dirt. Add to large pot filled with water and bring to boil. Boil until when you pierce a potato with fork it goes in easily, about 45 minutes. Do NOT overcook because they will continue to cook when you sauté them. NOTE: you can do this the night before by resting cooked potatoes on large cookie sheet. Cool, cover and refrigerate. When ready to finish cooking, peel potatoes and slice lengthwise about ½ inch thick. If slice is too long, cut it in half. Using large skillet, heat peanut oil (put in enough oil to reach about half way up potato slices). Meanwhile have a dinner plate filled with sugar. Dip the slices thoroughly in sugar, and sauté in peanut oil until browned on both sides. As they finish, put on non-stick foil lined cookie sheet. These can be made the night before, covered with foil and refrigerated or prepared same day, covered and left out at room temperature. When ready to serve, uncover and heat through in oven until bubbly.

SEAL AND SOAK VEGGIES

- *Broccoli florets*
- *Cauliflower florets*
- *Red pepper cut in chunks*
- *Yellow pepper cut in chunks*
- *Red onion cut in bite size pieces*
- *Sugar Snap Peas cut in half if they're big*
- *(pick any veggies you like that don't brown)*

Marinade:

- *1 can tomato soup*
- *½ cup cooking oil*
- *1 tsp. dry mustard*
- *½ tsp. pepper*
- *1-cup sugar¾ cup white vinegar1 tsp. salt1 tsp. Worcestershire sauce1 tsp. minced garlic*

This is one of those recipes that I've had for over 20 years, made it often and then forgot about it, completely. My mom unearthed it and thanked me after she made it for Rosh Hashanah dinner in Florida. She reminded me that I gave it to her years ago and when she told me the main ingredient, it all became clear and I was shocked I'd forgotten about it. It's an easy, make ahead recipe that is a true crowd pleaser.

In 2-gallon (x-large) size plastic bag mix all marinade ingredients. Put all cut veggies in bag, seal it up and shake it up. Whenever you open the fridge, move the bag around a little or flip it over so that marinade is soaking into and onto all the veggies. They will be ready to serve after resting overnight in the fridge. Take the veggies out of bag with slotted spoon so any reserve liquid stays in bag, not on your serving platter.

HONEY CAKE

- 5 eggs
- ½ cup oil
- 1 lb. honey
- 1-cup coffee
- 1 orange
- 1 lemon
- ¼ amoretto brandy (optional)
- 2-cups sugar
- 1-cup raisins
- 2 tsp. baking powder
- 5 cups sifted flour
- 2 tsp. baking soda
- 1 tsp. allspice
- 1 tsp. cloves
- 1 tsp. nutmeg
- 1-cup chopped nuts

My grandma Dorothy made this honey cake and it was always a special treat on Rosh Hashanah in which we celebrate the sweetness of apples and honey as a tribute to the Jewish new year. The recipe I have of hers was typed on a typewriter in which her all errors were xxx'd out. She also made this recipe is a large roasting pan to bake. To adapt, I use two 9x13 pans. I suppose this recipe is timeless. Enjoy.

In electric mixer, cream eggs, sugar, honey and coffee. Add baking soda, oil, flour, baking powder and raisins. Add grated orange and lemon along with the juice of each. Add the allspice, cloves, nutmeg and chopped nuts to batter. Grease baking pan thoroughly. Line pan with a cut open brown bag from grocery store. The paper will absorb the grease and keep cake from sticking to pan. Pour batter into large roasting pan and bake in a 325-degree oven for approximately an hour or until cake is nicely browned. Let cool before cutting cake.

MEXICAN FIESTA – ROSY HUGENER

Rosy Hugener was born and raised in Mexico and moved to the United States in her 20s. Since then she has hosted numerous successful Mexican parties, bringing together ingredients easy to find in the U.S. with an authentic Mexican kitchen. In this chapter you will learn how to host a Mexican fiesta for more than 30 people, including tips of how to make simple sugar free margaritas and which salsas, tortillas, tequilas and condiments to buy from your nearest supermarket or favorite website.

PREPARATION

Weeks before the party

Buy the tequila. For a party of around 30 people you will likely need three bottles of tequila. The first two will be for mixing, so they can be relatively inexpensive, but be sure to buy tequila that says "100% Agave." Reasonably priced brands that I recommend include Blue or Cazadores.

The third bottle of tequila will be for drinking straight. High quality white tequilas include Patron or Don Julio. For a more traditional Mexican sipping tequila, I recommend the reposado (rested) or añejo (aged) varieties of the brands Herradura and Don Julio. These are colored a golden brown and will likely cost $45-50 per bottle.

Think about the ingredients you will need for the recipes you will prepare. If any items are not available in your local supermarket, look into using one of these websites:

- www.thelatinproducts.com
- www.mexgrocer.com
- www.mymexicanpantry.com

Two days before the party – Shopping Day

Buy all ingredients two days before the party. Here are some hints on the produce:

Be sure to wrap the cilantro with absorbent paper such as a paper towel to keep it moist.

Leave onions and tomatoes outside the refrigerator; try to buy hard tomatoes, as squishy ones create too much liquid when you chop them

If your avocados are already a bit soft, put them in the refrigerator. If they are hard, leave them outside. It can take up to 3 days for an avocado to get to the right level of softness. To accelerate this process you can wrap them in brown paper, but be sure to check them periodically so they do not get overly, which will cause them to turn black in the middle.

One day before the party

Look through the recipes you intend to use for items called out as needed one day before the party and prepare those as described.

Buy colorful flowers and set them in flower vases.

Set tables and move chairs. Take out all the serving dishes and be sure that you have serving spoons for each dish. Use boxes wrapped in colorful paper to create layers for the tables, making sure that the boxes are strong enough to support the plates. Set out plates, cups and any other individual serving items you intend to use.

Prepare a good mix of dance music, for a Mexican fiesta must have dancing. Include Shakira, Carlos Santana, Enrique Iglesias and Pitbull in the mix. If you want other authentic music include some songs from Mana, Julieta Venegas and Juanes.

The day of the party

Give yourself enough time to cook all the recipes! For example, if your party is at 5 p.m., you will need to start cooking early that morning. But leave the guacamole to be done half an hour before people come if you want it to stay fresh.

Buy ice two hours before the party and put it in two coolers, one with just ice and one with bottles of soda, diet soda and Mexican beer (Corona, Corona Light, Negra Modelo and Victoria).

DRINKS

For each the key beverages of my party, I like to fill a large beverage jar with spigot in advance so that I will not have to worry about mixing drinks during the party. You can also use a crystal punch bowl. Either way, put the drinks next to a cooler of ice and let the guests serve themselves.

DIET MARGARITA OR PALOMA

- 1 liter bottle of Diet Squirt or Fresca.
- ¼ bottle of tequila
- The juice of 4 limes
- Splenda to sweeten the drink to your taste
- Lime cut in small slices to garnish

Any good Margarita needs a glass rimmed in either salt or chile powder. Supply cut limes for people to wet the glass rims and plates of kosher salt and the chile powder in which the glasses can be dipped. There is no need for more expensive "margarita salt," as coarse kosher salt works just fine. Also note that chile powder is a Mexican fruit seasoning, NOT chili powder. My favorite brands are (in order): Valetina, Tajin, Klass, Miguelito.

Combine everything in a large beverage jar and serve over ice.

REGULAR MARGARITA: (FOR A PITCHER)

- *The juice of 20 limes*
- *¼ bottle of Cointreau or another orange liqueur*
- *¼ bottle of tequila*
- *1 cup of white sugar syrup (to taste)*
- *Lime cut in small slices to garnish*
- *4 cups of water*

Mix all the ingredients in a medium size pitcher and serve over ice

Note: Sugar, Spenda and alcohol are to taste.

SOFT DRINKS

If you want to add Mexican soft drinks, here are my favorites: Sangria Señorial (sangria soda without alcohol), Sidral Mundet (apple soda), Jarritos mandarina and mango drink (This brand has many different fruit flavors, so try several)

FOOD

TINGA TOSTADAS

For Family dinner divide by 3.

- *15 Chicken breasts*
- *2 bunches of fresh cilantro*
- *1 onion to cook with the chicken*
- *10 onions cut in slices*
- *4 garlic cloves to cook with the chicken*
- *Sea salt*
- *2 cups of Olive oil*
- *4 Chopped Romaine lettuce heads*
- *6 bags of tostadas (hard, flat, round tortillas) -- any brand is fine*
- *2 bags of shredded manchego cheese, mozzarella or Mexican Mix cheese*
- *3 cups of refried beans (You may buy these, but if you choose to make your own here's how: boil black beans for 1 hour with salt. Add ½ cup of very finely chopped onion and 1 cup of olive oil. Puree in a food processor and return to the pot in which the beans were boiled. Mix for 5 minutes on low hear, adding salt to taste)*
- *2 cups of sour cream. Brands: La Chona or El Mexicano. You can buy American brands of sour cream but the Mexican brands have a better texture for spreading on the tostadas*
- *2 cans of chipotle in adobo sauce. My favorite brands are: La Costeña, Embasa or Herdez*
- *9 heirloom tomatoes (or other tomatoes if necessary)*

To do one day before the party:

1. Fill a large soup pot half way with water. Bring the water to a boil, then add the chicken, onion, cilantro and garlic. Add 3 soup spoons of sea salt.

2. Cook for about ½ hour. Discard the broth. Let the chicken cool down for about 1 hour and then shred it, removing any fat and leftover pieces of cilantro and onion.

3. Put the chicken in the refrigerator inside a closed container.

To do the morning of the party:

1. Remove all tostadas from their packages and place them in baskets lined with cloth napkins. Cover the baskets with food wrap.

2. Transfer the sour cream and shredded cheese to serving dishes, wrap them and put them back in the refrigerator.

3. Clean and shred the lettuce, put it in a serving bowl and cover in plastic wrap. If you have space in the refrigerator put it in the refrigerator; otherwise, you can leave it at room temperature.

To do 4 ½ hours before the party:

1. Sauté the onions in a large frying pan until the color changes from bright white to transparent white, then add the shredded chicken and stir five minutes.

2. Use a food processor to mix one can of chipotle with 2 tomatoes. Add the mix to the chicken, continuing to stir. Repeat with the second can of chipotle and two more tomatoes. Continue to add pureed tomatoes until the chicken (Tinga) is red but not runny. Salt to taste (perhaps up to two tablespoons).

3. Move the chicken to a buffet plate and leave outside to cool (about 90 minutes). Cover with food wrap and put in the refrigerator.

To do 30 minutes before the party:

Move the Tinga chicken from the refrigerator to a slow cooker or a sterno. Lay out the components of the tostadas in this order: tostadas, refried beans, Tinga chicken, lettuce, sour cream and cheese. Cut some tomatoes in slices to garnish the tostada. Your guests assemble their own tostadas to their individual tastes.

For Family dinner divide by 3.

SALPICON

To do one day before the party:

Fill a large soup pot half-way with water and bring to a boil. Add the flank steak, a whole onion, the bay leaves and the pepper. Add plenty of salt to flavor the meat. Boil for 90 minutes or until the flank steak is easy shredded. Remove the flank steak, strain all water and other material, and let stand for one hour.

Clean off any fat, shred the meat, and refrigerate.

To do the morning of the party:

Remove the shredded meat from the refrigerator. Clean off any fat that you see. Mix the flank steak with the onions, cilantro, radish and lime juice and salt to taste. Move the mixture to a serving dish, cover, and place in the refrigerator until 10 minutes before the party.

This dish should be served cold or at room temperature and can be eaten alone or on top of tostadas.

- 3 pounds of flank steak (with as little fat as possible)
- 1 whole onion
- 3 onions, finely chopped
- 6 bay leaves
- 1 teaspoon of ground pepper
- 3 bunches of radish, finely chopped (roots only)
- The juice of 5 limes
- Sea salt
- 3 bunches of finely chopped cilantro

TAMAL CAKE

- Tamale flour dry mix. Brand: Maseca "Masa para tamales"
- 1 cup of olive oil
- 5 poblano peppers
- 1 bag of Manchego chesse.
- 2 Table spoons of chicken broth bouillon (Knorr Suiza) or 3 chicken bouillon cubes
- 2 cups of water

To do the morning of the party:

Follow the instructions on the box of Tamale flour to make the dough, but use olive oil instead of lard. Note: do not buy the ready-made dough, as the flavor is a little different.

Place the chiles poblanos directly on the flames of your stove or grill until each side has turned mostly black. Under the faucet, remove the outside layer of burned skin, then pull out the heart of the chile (attached to the stem and filled with small seeds). Try to clean the veins of the chile (which are the spiciest part). Clean until no seeds are left, then chop into small pieces.

Put olive oil and the already-made dough into a frying pan and move constantly for about 5 minutes to start cooking the dough.

Grease and flour a cake pan (I use a Bundt pan) and add a one-inch layer of the heated dough. On top of this add one layer of the chile slices and a small layer of the cheese, then top with another one-inch layer of dough.

Boil the water in a pot and add the chicken bouillon to make a light soup. Ladle the soup over the preparation in the cake pan until liquid covers the dough. Cover the cake pan with aluminum foil and bake for 30 minutes or until a tooth pick inserted into the cake comes out clean and dry.

Leave the cake in the pan until one hour before the party, but be sure not to leave it uncovered or your cake will become dry and hard.

GUACAMOLE

- 6 avocados
- ½ onion, finely chopped
- 1 bunch of cilantro, finely chopped
- 2 limes
- 3 Serrano chiles, finely chopped
- 2 table spoons of salt or to taste.
- 2 bags of tortillas chips. I like to buy tortilla chips that are homemade at my local supermarket, but packaged brands such as Tostitos whole grain chips are fine as well

To do the morning of the party:

Chop all the ingredients and leave them outside the refrigerator in a closed container.

To do 30 minutes before the party:

Scoop out the flesh of the avocados and mix with the other ingredients. For a more rustic look, using a fork to mix the ingredients will leave some chunks of avocado. For a fancier look use a food processor to mix the ingredients thoroughly.
.

The guacamole will not stay green for long. Keep a spoon in the guacamole and be sure to stir it every half hour during the party.

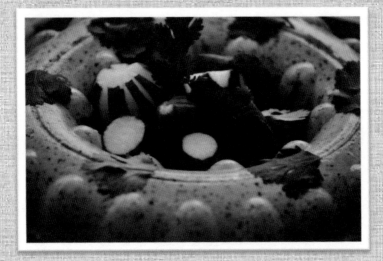

GUACAMOLE MOUSSE

- 1 block of Philadelphia (or other) cream cheese
- 2 table spoons of mayonnaise
- Olive oil or mayonnaise for greasing the container
- 3 avocados
- ¼ cup of boiling water
- The juice of 2 limes
- 2 envelopes of Knox unflavored gelatin
- 1 bunch of cilantro, finely chopped
- ½ of a small onion, finely chopped
- Salt
- Jel-Ring Tupperware mold or any small cake container

Unlike regular guacamole, this dish will not darken during your party.

1. Mix all the ingredients except the gelatin in a food processor. Dissolve the gelatin in ¼ cup of boiling water (should take only a few seconds), making sure that it is fully dissolved into a smooth liquid. Add this to the mix of ingredients.

2. Spread the mayonnaise or olive oil into the mold. Pour in the mix, then refrigerate for at least 3 hours.

3. Transfer the mousse from the mold to a plate 30 minutes before the party. If the mousse sticks to the container, submerge in hot water for few seconds and try again.

The mousse should be eaten as a spread on crackers

Angelos, Kokonis,Skordilis, Gekas, Alexacos, Panagakis and Psaltis
Karkazis and Vainikos not in the picture.

THE GREEK KITCHEN

CHRISTINA GALANIS ANGELOS, EVA SKORDILIS, JULIE KOKONIS PHIPPS, MARY PANAGAKIS, GEORGENE KARKAZIS SHANLEY, CONSTANCE GEKAS HUGDAHL, ALEXANDRA VAINIKOS CARSO, DIMITRA ALEXAKOS AND MIA PSALTIS CONNOLLY

A collection of traditional dishes inspiring a new generation

This chapter could not be made possible without the contributors been passionate about our culture and cuisine. Many of us grew up at watching and observing our mother, aunt or *yiayia*, preparing beautiful rustic food that fed the restless soul of the immigrant life. Far away from their familial homes and culture the early immigrants always prepared dishes that kept them connected. As keepers of our heritage it is important that we take the time to pass on these recipes to the next generation.

A big thank you to everyone who made this chapter possible and through this created new friendships.

THE GREEK PANTRY

Olive Oil the third largest producer of Olive oil in the world, the consumption of Olive oil is high in Greece mainly in part to the touted benefits of the "Mediterranean diet". Greece has in the past few years started to increase export of organic olive oil and thus made it more readily available to everyone.

Cheese

> *Like olives, nuts, preserved seafood and pickled vegetables are something you can just serve without much preparation. Cheese is a major component as part of a "meze" plate. Among them the following are the most popular:*

- **Feta cheese** is universally known as a classic Greek cheese. It is mainly made from sheep or goats milk and or combination of both. It ranges in flavor from soft and creamy to hard and pungent.
- **Kefalotiri or Kefalograviera** are both hard cheeses and are made from either sheep or goat milk. Hard grating cheeses, both are also good table cheeses although kefalograviera is used for both frying and grilling.
- **Mitzithra** is one of the oldest and simplest cheeses in Greece and most common in the Aegean islands. When fresh this whey cheese is eaten as a soft table cheese – closely resembling freshly made ricotta. It is used in pies and pastries. When aged and heavily salted it goes hard and is finely grated and served on top of pasta.

Olives are a mainstay of daily Greek meals. Most rural families still make their own olives and they are preserved in salt brine. Their color always depends on when they were picked and their state of ripeness. Green means they were picked at an early stage, purple to black means they were picked at a later stage of ripeness. The best know Greek olive is the Kalamata olive. All types of olives can be seasoned according to personal taste. Kalamata olives goe well with such herbs as thyme, savory and oregano. Green olives can be spiked with crushed coriander and or hot pepper flakes.

Fresh and Dried Herbs are widely used in the Greek kitchen. Mint, dill, parsley and wild fennel are the most widely used fresh herbs. The most prevalent dried herb is oregano, which tends to grow wild through various regions in Greece – it is always used dried in the Greek kitchen. Dried mint is the preferred seasoning in meatballs.

Spices are an integral part of Greek cooking and run the gamut of been used in both sweet and savory dishes. Allspice, cinnamon, cloves and nutmeg are used in the making of béchamel sauce, stews and meat sauces. Cumin is added to soutzoukakia and stifatho. Fennel seeds are mainly used when making homemade sausage, pickles, bread and some fish and pork stews.

Capers grow wild on most of the Greek Islands, especially on the Cyclades Islands. They are a staple of every household pantry; capers are picked in the summer months in the early evening when the flowers close and the insects are less bothersome. They are usually pickled and used as a condiment, and the larger ones are picked and boiled and served as a salad with olive oil and lemon.

Tarama is the fish roe from carp. It is used to make the classic meze taramosalata. It is usually a light pale color and is very flavorful without being overpowering.

Yogurt is used for marinades, sauces, cakes, pies and savory dishes. It is also a common dessert and breakfast in many parts of Greece, served simply with walnuts drizzled with honey and a dusting of cinnamon.

Vinegars made from wine are an indispensable part of the Greek kitchen since ancient times. It is the unami factor in meat and game stews especially in stifatho (traditionally made with rabbit), it imparts an important flavoring.

You will find all these staples of The Greek Kitchen in any of the International Markets in your local areas.

MEZE - APPETIZERS

TZATZIKI – GREEK YOGHURT DIP

- 1-2 medium seedless cucumber, peeled and finely chopped
- 1 – 2 tsp. white wine vinegar
- ½ pt. plain strained Greek yogurt
- ½ pt. sour cream
- ½ tsp. salt
- 1 tsp. chopped fresh dill
- ¼ tsp. garlic powder
- 2 Tbsp. olive oil

Recipe contributed by Christina Galanis Angelos

This is a very versatile dip that can be enjoyed with broiled chicken or fish. In Greece it is always added to one of the most popular street food snacks, souvlaki or gyros.

1. Combine all of the ingredients and mix together. Place in the refrigerator to chill before serving. This can be used as a dip for vegetables, grilled meat, served with pita bread, or on a sandwich.

2. Fage Greek yogurt works really well for this dish, as it is already strained and will provide the correct consistency.

Note – to minimize the strong garlic aftertaste, simply crush the garlic with a mortar and pestle before adding the other ingredients.

TARAMA – FISH ROE DIP

Recipe contributed by Georgene Karkazis Shanley

- 1 jar 10 oz. Tarama – smoked cod roe
- 1 med. size white onion- grated
- ¼ cup white vinegar
- 6 Tables lemon juice
- ¼ tsp. sugar
- 3 1/4 C. Mazola oil
- 10 slices white bred

Taramosalata is eaten widely during the Lenten period. It is a staple in many Greek kitchens and is always enjoyed as part of a meze platter.

1. Remove the crusts from the bread and soak in water for about 10-15 minutes, squeeze all the excess water and put to the side.

2. Mix together the lemon juice and vinegar.

3. Place the Tarama in a cuisinart and beat until soft and fluffy , then start adding the ,oil a little at a time, alternating with the vinegar/lemon juice , until you have a nice fluffy mixture . Once you start getting a nice fluffy consistency you can start adding the moistened bread slices and grated onion.

Refrigerate until ready to use and allow the flavors to develop. Serve with pita, crusty bread or crackers

Note: Kronos brand Tarama is preferred for this recipe

SKORTHALIA – GARLIC DIP

Recipe contributed by Eva Skordilis

- *4 large Idaho potatoes*
- *1 head of garlic*
- *6 tbsp extra virgin olive oil*
- *4 tbsp white vinegar*
- *Salt to taste*

If you like garlic then this is the dip for you. It is traditionally made with potatoes, but in some regions of Greece it is made with bread. It is always eaten with fried fish or vegetables, like zucchini, eggplant, warm boiled beets or wild greens.

1. Peel and boil potatoes until fork tender. Drain from hot water and allow potatoes to cool before mashing.

2. Crush garlic to a paste and place in a bowl with potatoes, olive oil, and vinegar. Using a hand mixer on low combine the ingredients until they are smooth like mashed potatoes.

3. Careful not to over mix because the potatoes will become paste like.

4. Salt to taste.

5. Serve with fresh bread or pita bread.

MELITZANOSALATA -EGGPLANT DIP

Recipe contributed by Eva Skordilis

- 3 large eggplants
- ½ of a large onion
- 2 garlic cloves, crushed
- Juice of one lemon
- 7 tbsp extra virgin olive oil
- Salt and Pepper – to taste
- flat leaf parsley
- 1 diced roasted red pepper (optional)

The eggplant is one of the most versatile vegetables in the world. The Greek's affinity for using it in so many ways, knows no bounds. Here is one way that this versatile vegetable can be enjoyed as part of a meze platter.

1. Preheat oven to 350 F, Prick the eggplants and place them on a cooking sheet lined with parchment paper. Place in oven for about one hour or until soft.

2. When the eggplants cool, cut them in half and spoon the flesh into a food processor and add the onion, garlic and lemon juice. Season with salt and pepper and process until smooth.

3. With the motor running drizzle in the olive oil. Taste and adjust any additional seasonings or lemon.

4. Cover and chill for 1 hour to develop the flavor.

5. Garnish with finely chopped flat leaf parsley just before serving.

6. Serve with fresh bread or pita bread.

TYROPITA IN A PUFF

Recipe contributed by Mary Panagakis

Tyropita or cheese pies abound in every corner bakery and are a go-to snack for Greeks on a daily basis. They are traditionally eaten as a meze and are considered universal street food like its other best-known cousin spanakopita. Here is a recipe which puts a twist on a very traditional meze.

- 1 ½ lb. Greek feta
- ½ lb. large curd cottage cheese (4% milk fat)
- 5 eggs
- 8oz cream cheese – room temperature
- 2 packets frozen puffed pastry sheets

1. Preheat oven to 400º
2. In a large bowl beat the cream cheese until softened. Add the eggs and beat until combined. Add the feta cheese which has been broken up into small crumbs (you still want to maintain texture – best to break up with your hands), Add the cottage cheese into the mix.
3. Blend gently so the mixture remains chunky.
4. At this time bring the puffed pastry out of the freezer and remove from the packaging. Separate sheets and place on cookie sheet. You should have 6 sheets.
5. With a large spoon, scoop the mixture down the length of every other puffed pastry sheet. You will have 3 sheets topped with the mixture and three sheets that will be plain. The plain pastry sheets will be used to cover the ones with the mixture.
6. Press the puffed pastry around the edges with a fork to seal in the mixture.
7. Bake for 30 minutes or until golden brown. Remove from oven and cool before serving.

DOLMADES – STUFFED GRAPE LEAVES

Recipe contributed by Julie Kokonis Phipps

- 2 cups Arborio rice
- 2 medium onions
- 1 cup olive oil
- 3 Tbs. flat leaf parsley
- 3 Tbs. fresh dill
- 3 Tsp. fresh mint
- 2 lemons
- 1 jar grape leaves, in brine
- 1 tsp salt and ½ tsp pepper

Dolmades stuffed with rice are usually enjoyed as a meze served on their own and or enjoyed with tzatziki. They can also be stuffed with ground pork and beef and served with a classic avgolemono sauce, for a heartier meal. Dolmades are typically served with lemon wedges and can be accompanied with a Greek yogurt dip. In Greece, grape leaves first appear on the vines in spring and early summer, and they are usually picked just days after appearing, to ensure their tenderness.

1. In a small pot, bring water and a dash of olive oil to a boil. Remove from the heat. Gently separate the grape leaves, and drain off any excess brine. Place them in the boiling water for a few minutes to soften. If using fresh grape leaves, cut the stems off, wash the leaves well, and blanch in boiling water. Remove the leaves from the water and place them on a plate to cool before stuffing.

2. Place the Arborio rice along with finely diced onions, parsley, dill and mint in a bowl. Add the olive oil along with the salt and pepper.

4. Place 4 grape leaves on the bottom of a large pot. This provides a barrier of protection minimizing the chances of scorching the dolmades.

5. Then take a grape leaf and place it, shiny side down, on your countertop. You need to have the underside with the visible branching facing you, ready to be topped with the rice mixture.

6. Place a heaping teaspoon of the rice mixture at the base of the grapevine . Fold over the two sides of the grape leaf to hold in the filling, and then roll in a tight and firm fashion – just like a burrito. The shiny side of the leaf should be showing. Place the stuffed dolmades in the pot, in neat circular layers. Place any remaining unstuffed grape leaves on top of the dolmades to stop them from moving while cooking.

7. Cover the dolmades with an upside-down plate. This also helps prevent the dolmades from moving and breaking apart while they are cooking. Add enough water to the pot, almost covering the dolmades. Drizzle olive oil around the bowl and bring to a boil. Then lower the heat to a medium simmer for about an hour and half – until the rice is cooked.

8. Keep an eye on the liquid, if it looks like it is been readily absorbed add a little more to aid the cooking process if needed.

SPANAKOPITA – SPINACH PIE

Recipe contributed by Georgene Karkazis Shanley

Spanakopita is the universal snack in Greece, enjoyed on the run and enjoyed as a late morning snack.

- 2 lb spinach - frozen
- 1 lb butter- melted
- 1 bunch of green onions - chopped
- 1 lb. crumbled Greek Feta cheese
- salt and freshly ground pepper to taste
- 7 eggs
- fresh dill to taste (optional)
- 1 box filo pastry sheets #4

1. Thaw spinach and squeeze excess water or wash and chop fresh spinach and place in big bowl.

2. Add chopped green onions, feta, eggs, salt, pepper (to taste) and ¾ cup melted butter. Take filo sheet and lightly brush melted butter all over the sheet. Place second to overlap on top of first sheet. Butter each sheet up to 6 –7 sheets over lapping one another. Do not place sheets directly on top of each other, they must be staggering.

3. Take a big spoon full of spinach filling and place it along the last piece of butter filo. Make sure the filling covers the whole length of filo. Fold side of the filo up to the spinach and start rolling the filo/spinach mixture into a log form. Brush top of log with butter and place on cookie sheet to bake. This recipe will make up to 4-5 logs depending on how much spinach mixture you put on the filo.

4. You may pre-score the top of the log so it is easier to cut after it has baked. Bake at 350F for 30 min until golden brown. If you make the logs and freeze them before you cook them, the cooking time will take longer. Maybe up to 1 hour to cook, so plan ahead on time

KEFTETHES – GREEK MEATBALLS

Recipe contributed by Christina Galanis Angelos

- 1 lb. ground beef
- 2-3 slices day old bread
- milk
- 1 large onion
- 1 Tbsp. fresh mint
- 2 Tbsp. flat leaf parsley
- 1 tsp. salt
- ½ tsp. pepper
- 1/3 cup red wine
- 2 eggs
- 1 cup flour
- Canola oil for Frying

Keftedes or fritters can be almost made from anything. The beef keftedes are the most well known and are enjoyed with a squeeze of lemon, some dip and a sip of ouzo.

1. Place the ground beef, coarsely grated onion, finely chopped fresh mint and parsley along with salt, pepper and red wine in a bowl .
2. Remove crust from bread, break up into chunks and add a little milk to soak and reconstitute. When it has reconstituted squeeze excess liquid and add it to the beef mixture. Use your hands to gently combine all the ingredients.
3. Cover and chill for 1 hour.
4. Flour your hands. Shape into balls and roll lightly into the flour. Heat a large fry pan , add enough canola oil to cover the bottom and then fry the meat balls until brown. Place on a platter with a paper towel to absorb any excess oil from the meat balls.
4. Serve them plain or with a tomato sauce

Note: The meatballs can also be baked by placing them on a cookie sheet lined with parchment paper at 350 degrees for about 15-20 minutes.

SOUPS

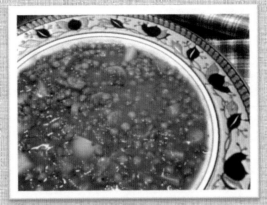

LENTIL SOUP

Recipe contributed by Alexandra Vainikos Carson

- *1 cup lentils – brown lentils*
- *4 cups water*
- *1 onion - chopped*
- *2 stalks celery*
- *2 carrots -chopped*
- *1 potato -chopped*
- *1 clove garlic, minced*
- *1 bay leaf*
- *2 tblsp fresh flat leaf parsley*
- *1/2 cup olive oil*
- *1/2 cup tomato sauce*
- *salt to taste*

Pulses are widely used the Greek Kitchen. In Greece brown lentils are used to make this very traditional soup whose recipe has remained unchanged since ancient times. It is eaten extensively during periods of religious fasting, such as Lent.

1. Place lentils in a bowl and wash under cold water removing black pieces or twigs, drain.

2. In a medium pan simmer lentils in warm water with onion, celery, carrot, potato, garlic, bay leaf, parsley and oil. Cook until lentils are tender, about an hour.

In the last 15 minutes of cooking add tomato sauce and salt to taste.

Note: you can also make this soup using puy lentils – they hold their shape really well and have a much more delicate and nuttier flavor.

AVGOLEMONO SOUP – EGG LEMON SOUP

Recipe contributed by Eva Skordilis

- 8 cups chicken stock
- ¾ cup orzo pasta
- 2 eggs - room temperature
- ¼ cup lemon juice
- Salt and pepper to taste

A classic comfort soup in any kitchen, this is standard fare in Greek restaurants. Purists will make it with white rice, however the more delicate texture of orzo pasta lends itself well to this soup.

1. Pour stock into pot and bring up to boil. Add the pasta and continue to boil for about 8 minutes. Continue to stir so the pasta does not stick to the bottom of the pot. Once the pasta has cooked remove from heat. Add lemon juice to the soup.

2. Place eggs in a mixing bowl – mix with hand mixer until the mixture is smooth and bubble. Remove one cup of hot broth from soup and slowly add to egg mixture while mixing with hand mixer. This step is crucial that it is done correctly because you are "tempering" the egg mixture to come to temperature with the soup so that you do not end up with scrambled egg.

3. Once the egg mixture has been tempered, return the egg mixture into pot, stirring over low heat to incorporate the avgolemono well and until soup thickens – 2 to 3 minutes. Stirring constantly.

4. Remove from heat, check for seasoning and let stand for 5 minutes before serving.

FASOLADA – BEAN SOUP

Recipe contributed by Eva Skordilis

- 2 cups dried Navy Beans or Cannellini Beans
- 15 cups cold water - divided
- 1/4 cup olive oil
- 1 tbsp butter
- 1 diced white onion
- 2 cups each celery and carrots
- 2 bay leaves
- Salt and Pepper to taste
- Juice of one lemon

A classic vegetarian soup that is simple and hearty. This soup is a mainstay in the Greek army diet. It is enjoyed with crusty bread and good company.

1. Rinse beans in cold running water and place in pot with 6 cups of water. Once they come to a boil remove from heat, cover pot, and let beans soak for 1 to 1 ½ hours. Alternatively you can soak bean overnight in cold water.

2. Drain and rinse the beans.

3. In a soup pot heat olive oil and butter – once the butter has melted stir in onions, celery and carrots and sauté for 3 to 4 minutes. Add salt and pepper. Then add 9 cups of water, beans and bay leaves and bring to boil. Reduce heat and simmer for 1 ½ hours or until the beans are tender

4. Remove from heat and add additional salt and pepper to taste along with the juice of one lemon.

SIDE DISHES

GREEK PEAS

Recipe contributed by Alexandra Vainikos Carson

- ¼ cup Bertolli Extra Light Olive Oil
- 1 small onion
- 14.5oz. can whole plum tomato
- 1 lb. frozen peas
- ¼ cup fresh dill, finely chopped
- Salt & pepper to taste

This is a very seasonal dish served in tavernas. It can be enjoyed on its own with some feta cheese and crusty bread.

1. Sauté onion in oil until translucent. Roughly chop the whole and add them to the onions along with the tomato puree in the can.
2. Add the frozen peas along with the chopped dill, salt and pepper. Stir to combine, bring to medium simmer and cook peas until tender.
3. Enjoy with some crusty bread and Greek cheese like feta or kefalograviera.

Options:
Add mushrooms or artichokes

GREEN BEANS

Recipe contributed by Mary Panagakis

This dish can be enjoyed with heartier meat dishes, and is quite popular in the summer months when the beans are fresh and seasonal. During periods of fasting they are a mainstay in the Greek Kitchen.

- 2 lbs. fresh green beans
- 1 onion – finely chopped or coarse grated
- 4oz can tomato sauce
- 1 cup water
- Salt and pepper to taste
- ½ tsp. garlic powder
- 1 tbs. fresh dill
- 1/3 cup olive oil

1. Top and tail the fresh beans, rinse well in cold water, if they are too big you can cut them in half of thirds.

2. In a medium saucepan place the green beans, the chopped/grated onion, the cup of water and the tomato sauce. Then add all the seasonings and stir to combine. Olive oil should be added last and drizzled over everything.

3. Cover the saucepan bring to a boil then reduce heat to a simmer, cook until tender for approx. 45 minutes or until the beans are cooked.

4. Spoon the green beans into a platter and serve warm.

SPANAKORIZO – SPINACH RICE

Recipe contributed by Julie Kokonis Phipps

With the addition of spinach, fresh herbs, and lemon, Spanakorizo is a healthy and tasty alternative to plain rice. In fact, Spanakorizo has become a favorite side dish of many Greek families.

- 3/4 cup rice – Uncle Bens
- 2 cups water
- 2 bags baby spinach
- Extra virgin olive oil
- 1 large onion - chopped
- 1/2 cup fresh dill - chopped
- 1 tsp. Contadina Italian Herbs tomato paste
- Juice of 1 lemon
- Salt and pepper to taste
- Feta cheese

1. In a large pot, sauté onion with olive oil until translucent, add spinach and stir until the spinach starts to wilt. Then add the fresh dill.

2. Add the tomato paste and stir to combine with the rest of ingredients for a few minutes. Add the rice and 2 cups of water, season with salt and pepper, stir to combine. Cover the saucepan and bring to a boil. Reduce to a simmer for about 20 minutes until the rice is cooked.

3. Once it has finished cooking remove from the heat and stir in the juice of one lemon. Allow to sit for about 10 minutes before gently fluffing with a fork.

4. Serve with your favorite feta cheese, grilled fish and or chicken.

GREEK POTATOES

- *3 lbs. baking potatoes*
- *1 ½ tsp. salt*
- *1 tsp. freshly ground pepper*
- *1 tsp. garlic powder*
- *2 tsp. Greek oregano*
- *¾ cup freshly squeezed lemon juice*
- *½ cup extra virgin olive oil*
- *1 cup water*

Recipe contributed by Mary Panagakis

A mainstay of tavernas, they are delicious in their simplicity.

1. Peel and slice the potatoes in wedges. Then place them in a 12x14 baking pan.
2. Add the water, lemon and olive oil. Sprinkle the seasonings over the potatoes and mix well.
3. Cover your pan with aluminum foil and bake at 400 degrees for 1 hour. For a nice golden brown color, uncover the last 10 minutes.
4. You can adjust the seasoning to taste.

GREEK SALAD – HORIATIKI SALATA

Recipe contributed by Dimitra Alexakos

- vine ripened tomatoes
- green or red bell pepper
- cucumber – seedless
- red onion
- kalamata olives
- greek feta cheese
- dried Greek oregano
- olive oil sea
- sea salt - Maldon

One of the best known and beloved dishes. This classic salad shines when you use good quality ingredients. In any taverna in Greece or Greek kitchen, this salad is standard fare and is always enjoyed with copious amounts of olive oil and crusty horiatiko bread to dip into the magical juices that are created from the tomatoes , oil and feta cheese.

1. Slice the tomato, cucumber and bell pepper into nice size portions. Add some thinly sliced red onion and toss to combine. Season sparingly with a little sea salt and dried oregano – to just give the tomato a lift.
2. Drizzle olive oil and garnish with chunks of feta cheese and kalamata olives to taste.
3. Enjoy with crusty bread.

BURNT BUTTER MACARONIA

Recipe contributed by Mia Psaltis Connolly

- *I lb thick spaghetti*
- *1 cup grated kefalograviera cheese*
- *1 stick butter*

The ultimate comfort food, the go to dish for harried cooks. The secret to this dish is burning and browning the butter – a good quality European butter is recommended for this dish as it tends to have a higher fat ratio that will let you achieve that delicate nutty flavor.

1. While the pasta is cooking place the butter in a small saucepan and melt on a low heat. You need to allow the foam to subside and then the butter will start to brown.
2. Drain the pasta well and place one third of the pasta on a platter, sprinkle some cheese and a little of the burnt butter, keep on "layering" the platter until all the pasta, cheese and butter have been used up.
3. Serve immediately.
Note: Thick style pasta is recommended for this dish. You can also use mytzithra, this cheese is always grated very finely, so season accordingly.

MAIN COURSE

ROASTED LEG OF LAMB

Recipe contributed by Mary Panagakis

- 5 to 7 lb. leg of lamb
- 4 cloves of garlic (halved)
- 1 Tbsp. salt
- 1 ½ tsp. freshly ground pepper
- 1 ½ tsp. garlic powder
- 3 Tbsp. olive oil

Apart from great religious or festive occasions, meat eating has always been a frugal affair in Greece. Easter is always celebrated with the paschal lamb and a soup called "mayeritsa" is made from the lamb's intestines and eaten first to break the Lenten fast. The classic roast lamb is a mainstay in any family gathering, along with Greek potatoes – what is there not to love about this meal .

1. Place the leg of lamb in a roasting pan and rub with the olive oil.
2. With a pointed knife make 8 slits on the lamb and fill with the halved garlic cloves.
3. Drizzle the olive oil over the lamb, mix the seasonings in a small bowl, and sprinkle over the lamb.
4. Cover and roast at 325º until meat is tender about 2 hours.

Note: Greeks tend to enjoy their lamb well done

PASTICHIO

Meat Sauce

- 2 Tbsp olive oil
- 1 onion chopped
- 3 lbs ground beef or lamb
- 1 cup red wine
- Salt and pepper
- ½ tsp cinnamon
- 1 cup tomato sauce
- 2 eggs slightly beaten
- 1 cup grated kefalotiri cheese or Romano cheese

Macaroni

- 1 lb macaroni, #5 or #6 – Misko brand or thick bucatini style pasta
- 2 eggs slightly beaten
- 1 stick melted butter
- 2 cups grated Kefalotiri cheese or Romano cheese

Recipe contributed by Eva Skordilis

This is a well known and beloved dish that is found throughout Greece. It may seem time consuming to make because there are a few stages – if you make the meat sauce in advance, then by the time you make the béchamel sauce and boil the pasta the dish comes together in no-time. It re-heats really well for any festive occasion.

Meat Sauce:1. In sauce pan heat olive oil and cook onions until tender add meat and brown well, stirring continuously. Remove any excess fat.

2. Add wine, salt, pepper, cinnamon and tomato sauce and simmer for about an hour until moisture evaporates. Check for seasoning and adjust if necessary.

3. Remove from heat and allow to cool for about 30 minutes. Then stir in the eggs and cheese.

Macaroni: 1. Boil macaroni for 15 minutes, Drain well and return to pot.

2. Combine eggs, butter and cheese, pour over macaroni and mix well.

Béchamel Sauce:1. Melt butter in sauce pan. Add flour and blend with whisk to make a roux. Cook for 2-3 minutes to take the rawness out of the flour. Gradually add the hot milk, whisking constantly until sauce has slightly thickened.

2. Allow the mixture to cool to lukewarm before adding the beaten eggs, cheese, salt and ground nutmeg. Stir well to combine. Check for seasoning and place to the side.

Béchamel Sauce

- 10 tbsp butter
- 10 tbsp flour
- 7 cups hot milk
- 4 eggs
- 1 cup grated kefalotiri cheese or Romano cheese
- 2 tsp salt
- Dash of ground nutmeg

Assembly:1. Preheat over to 350º.
2. Place the prepared macaroni in big bowl. Add one cup of the béchamel sauce and toss to combine. Then place in a 15" x 11" deep baking dish.
Spread meat sauce over the macaroni. At this point you can work the meat sauce into the macaroni slightly.
3. Spoon the rest of the béchamel sauce over the pasta meat dish. Drizzle with 2 tablespoons of melted butter and bake for 1 hour and 20 minutes or until golden brown.
4. Cool at least 30 minutes before serving.

BRIAMI
Recipe contributed by Mary Panagakis

- 4-5 Zucchini
- 2 Medium Size Eggplants
- 2 Lbs. Potatoes
- 1 tsp. salt1/2 tsp. freshly ground pepper
- ½ cup olive oil
- ¾ cup water½ tsp. garlic powder
- 4 oz. can tomato sauce

A very popular summertime dish that uses all the seasonal vegetables.
1. Wash vegetables. Cut zucchini, eggplants and potatoes into bite size pieces. Place mixed vegetables in a roasting pan. Cover with oil, water and tomato sauce. Season with salt and pepper and garlic powder and mix well.
2. Cover with foil and bake at 375º for 45 minutes. Uncover and bake for another 15 minutes or until golden brown.
Note: Can be served warm or cold.

MOUSSAKA

Recipe contributed by Eva Skordilis

Another dish that is renowned worldwide and considered a quintessential Greek dish. moussaka is traditionally make with eggplants, potatoes and meat sauce. Sometimes you will see it made with zucchini for lighter fare.

- 2 tbsp olive oil
- 1 diced onion
- 3 lbs ground sirloin or ground lamb
- 1 cup red wine
- 1 cup tomato sauce
- 4 tbsp fresh parsley chopped
- Dash of ground nutmeg
- Salt and freshly ground pepper
- 2 eggs
- ¼ cups grated Kefalotiri cheese or Romano cheese
- 8 medium eggplants
- 1/4 cups olive oil
- 3 Tbsp bread crumbs
- Béchamel recipe to followBéchamel sauce
- 10 Tbsp butter
- 10 Tbsp flour
- 7 cups hot milk
- 4 eggs
- 1 cup grated Kefalotiri cheese or Romano cheese
- 2 tsp salt
- Dash of ground nutmeg

1. Sauté 2 Tbsp olive oil with diced onion until they begin to sweat. Add meat and brown well stirring continuously. Add wine, tomato sauce, parsley, nutmeg, salt and pepper and continue to cook for about 30 minutes. Remove from heat and cool. Add eggs and cheese blend well and set aside.

2. Heat oven to 350°. Peel eggplants and slice about ½" pieces. Brush with olive oil and place on cookie sheets. Place in oven for about 30 minutes or until the eggplant becomes soft. Alternatively you can also grill them.

3. Grease a 15"x11" roasting pan and sprinkle with bread crumbs.

4. Arrange ½ of the eggplant slices closely together on bottom of pan. Spread meat mixture evenly over eggplants. Arrange remaining eggplants over meat mixture and cover with a thick layer of béchamel sauce.

5. Bake 50 minutes or until golden brown.

Sauce: 1. Melt butter in a sauce pan. Add flour and blend with whisk to make a roux cook for 2-3 minutes to take the rawness out of the flour. Gradually add the hot milk, whisking constantly until sauce has slightly thickened.

2. Allow the mixture to cool to lukewarm before adding the beaten eggs, cheese, salt and ground nutmeg. Stir well to combine. Check for seasoning and place to the side.

STIFATHO – BRAISED BEEF WITH ONIONS

Recipe contributed by Christina Galanis Angelos

- *3 lbs. boneless chuck*
- *4-5 lbs. small onions*
- *¼ cup olive oil*
- *¼ cup butter*
- *1 can crushed tomatoes*
- *¾ cup red wine vinegar*
- *3 cloves garlic minced*
- *2 bay leaves*
- *Salt and freshly ground pepper to taste*
- *1 cinnamon stick*

Traditionally this dish is made with rabbit or hare. The meat is marinated overnight before being braised with the baby onions, vinegar and spices . A classic one-pot stew this meal tastes so much better when enjoyed the next day. It reheats really well and should be enjoyed with a good crusty bread.

1. Cut the meat into small cubes and brown in olive oil. Add the garlic, cinnamon and the bay leaves and sauté until fragrant.

2. Add the crushed tomatoes, wine vinegar and stir to combine.

3. Meanwhile peel the small onions and leaving them whole and add to the meat.

4. Cover and bring to boil and then simmer for about 2 hours or until the meat is fork tender and the onions have softened.

5. Periodically check the stew during the cooking process and check to make sure there is enough braising liquid, if not add a little water.

6. Remove the cinnamon stick and bay leaf after cooking. Serve warm with a rice pilaf or pasta.

GREEK CHICKEN

Recipe contributed by Alexandra Vainikos Carson

- 1 whole chicken cut up
- 1/4 cup olive oil
- 1/4 cup corn oil
- 1 fresh lemon, squeezed (according to taste)
- 1 Tbsp greek oregano
- 1 Tsp granulated garlic powder
- salt and freshly ground pepper to taste

As in many kitchens around the world, chicken is considered a very versatile meat. In the Greek kitchen this is no exception. This recipe uses classic greek seasonings and the chicken is baked either in the oven or taken to the local bakery to roast in their ovens.

1. Preheat oven to 350°.
2. Wash chicken and pat dry. Place chicken in a roasting pan, skin side up. In a bowl combine olive oil, corn oil, lemon, oregano, garlic powder, salt and pepper. Stir until mixed and pour over chicken.
3. Roast until the chicken is cooked well, approximately one hour turning the chicken pieces over half way through the cooking process. Occasionally baste the chicken with juices collecting in the roasting pan.
4. When the chicken is done, turn on the broiler for 5 minutes to brown the chicken, turning the pieces over to each side, This will give the chicken a nice golden color.
Notes: Chicken can be marinated for up to two days. Pork Chops can be substituted for Chicken.

YEMISTA – STUFFED TOMATOES AND PEPPERS

Recipe contributed by Julie Kokonis Phipps

Stuffed tomatoes are a very typical and economical vegetarian meal that can be found at every local "taverna" in Greece. Not only does the author of this recipe remember eating them a lot in Greece as a child, but she also has fond memories of carrying her Grandmother's uncooked dishes of "Yemista" to the local bakery to be baked (which many locals did as well), as her Grandmother's kitchen was too small to accommodate a large oven. Meat lovers can add ground beef to the rice mixture.

- *A combination of tomatoes and green pappers to fit your pan (if you prefer, you may substitute with, baby eggplant or zucchini)*
- *2 large yellow onions, chopped*
- *olive oil*
- *1 bunch fresh flat leaf parsley, chopped*
- *1 bunch fresh mint, chopped*
- *1 handful of pine nuts*
- *1 ½ cups rice – Uncle Bens*
- *Breadcrumbs*
- *parmesan cheese*
- *serve with feta*

1. Turn the tomatoes upside down and cut the bottoms off to use as lids (green peppers don't need to be turned upside down before creating a lid). Scoop out the pulp of the tomatoes and put it in a bowl. Scoop out the seeds of the peppers and discard. Salt the insides of the tomatoes and peppers and place them in a baking pan. In a blender blend the tomato pulp- and put to the side.

2. Sauté the onions with olive oil until they become translucent. Add the rice, parsley, mint, pine nuts, ½ of the blended tomato pulp, and enough water to cover the rice. Cook until the rice is al dente. Turn off the heat and add salt, pepper and ½ cup parmesan cheese and combine well.

3. Fill the tomatoes and or peppers with the rice mixture to about ¾ full and cover the vegetables with their lids. Once you have filled all your vegetables and covered them with their lids pour the rest of the tomato pulp over them , drizzle with olive oil, and sprinkle with bread crumbs and parmesan cheese.

4. Add a little water to the pan and bake at 350° for 2 ½ hours, cover with tin foil for the last ½ hour or so.

SOUTZOUKAKIA SMIRNEIKA - MEATBALLS

Recipe contributed by Dimitra Alexakos

This is a famous "Greek" dish from Smyrna (modern day Izmir, Turkey) brought to the mainland in 1922 when Greeks in Asia Minor were forced to flee their homes. It can be found in most tavernas as a regular menu item. The meatballs can either be fried or baked in the oven and are always simmered in a tomato sauce.

- *2 slices white bread, crusts removed OR 4 tablespoons panko breadcrumbs*
- *1 pound ground beef – sirloin at least 90%*
- *1 med size onion peeled and grated*
- *3 cloves garlic – crushed*
- *1 tblsp finely chopped flat leaf parsley*
- *1 egg beaten*
- *2 teaspoons ground cumin*
- *Salt and freshly ground pepper*
- *All purpose flour for dredging*
- *Olive Oil for frying*

Tomato sauce:

- *1 can crushed tomatoes 28oz*
- *1 garlic clove finely diced*
- *1 teaspoon dried oregano*
- *Salt and freshly ground pepper*
- *Olive oil*

Tomato sauce: Heat a couple of tablespoons of olive oil, add the garlic and oregano and heat through until fragrant. Then add the crushed tomatoes and stir through. Allow to simmer for about 30 minutes – stirring occasionally. Place to the side and prepare the meatballs.

1. Preheat oven to 350º

2. Soak the bread or panko breadcrumbs in water for about 10-15 minutes, and then squeeze out all the excess moisture. Combine the bread, beef, onion, garlic, parsley, egg, cumin and seasoning in a bowl and mix to combine well with a light hand.

3. Shape into oval shaped meatballs, approximately 2 inches long, roll in the A.P. flour. Heat the oil in the fry pan and sauté the meatballs on all sides for about 5 minutes, until they form a slight crust and brown slightly.

4. Remove with a slotted spoon and place in a baking dish. Cover with the prepared tomato sauce and bake in the oven for 25 minutes, covered with aluminum foil.

5. Serve over plain white rice - jasmine rice. You can always thin out the sauce with a little water if it becomes too thick.

DESSERT

KOURAMBIEDES

Recipe contributed by Constance Gekas Hugdahl

- 1 pound unsalted butter
- ½ cup powdered sugar
- 2 teaspoons Mastiha
- 1 teaspoon vanilla essence
- 1 teaspoon orange juice
- 3 cups all purpose flour
- 1 packet powdered confectioners sugar

These cookies are traditionally served at Christmas and New Year. They are buttery and melt in your mouth. This is a family recipe that has been shared for the first time by our contributor Constance. Here is the story of the kourambiethes it deserves to be shared ......

"Yiayia Thomas (Thomopoulos) was originally from Kalamata. She came to America to live with her brother, who already lived in the states, when she turned 18. Though she came to America at 18, she had begun baking with her mother and her Yiayia since she was 10 years old. She married and had three children, and became a wonderful homemaker and baker. Anyone who tasted her goodies loved them! Her warmth and loving smile came with each batch of whatever she made. Her recipes have been handed down to the generations and have not been shared with anyone...until now! The kourambiethes bring a taste of her warmth and loving smile with each bite!"

1. Melt butter and beat for about 15 minutes. Add beaten egg yolk, powdered sugar, orange juice, vanilla and mastiha. Beat for 30 minutes – it gets creamier.

2. Add flour, adding a little at time until you get the right consistency (soft yet firm). Form into little balls and place on a baking sheet lined with parchment paper. Bake at 300º until cookie is light brown on the bottom.

3. Meanwhile cover a bench area with wax paper and or a large tray. Sift a layer of powdered sugar on the bench/tray. Once the cookies are baked remove them immediately from the baking sheet pan and place them on either the bench or tray close to each other.

4. Sift a thick blanket of powdered sugar onto the cookies. You will end up using the whole box of powdered sugar.

MELOMAKARONA

- 2 sticks unsalted butter
- 3 cups Mazola
- 3 egg yolks
- 1 ½ cups sugar
- 1 freshly squeezed orange
- 1 tsp. baking soda
- 2 tsps. baking powder
- 1 tsp. cinnamon
- ¼ tsp. ground cloves
- Swans Down cake flour (approx. 1 ½ boxes)

Syrup

- 2 cups honey
- 2 cups sugar
- 2 cups water
- 1 cinnamon stick
- ¼ fresh lemon
- 2 whole cloves
- 1 cup chopped walnuts (topping)

Recipe contributed by Mary Panagakis

Another cookie that is enjoyed over the Christmas and New Year festivities. It is a spicy cookie drenched in honey syrup , the perfect accompaniment to a cup of Greek coffee.

1. In a large bowl, cream the butter and sugar for 15-20 minutes. Then add the oil and egg yolks. Next combine the baking soda in the orange juice, before adding to the mix, with the rest of the ingredients. Stir in the flour and finish by kneading the dough until well blended. Dough should be soft and pliable.

2. Place a tablespoon of dough in the palm of your hand and squeeze slightly to form an oblong egg shape. Place on sheet pan, lined with parchment paper and make an indentation on top of the cookie crosswise, with the back of the fork. Bake at 350º for 20-22 minutes.

3. Bring honey, sugar and water to a boil, skiming the foam as needed. Add the cinnamon stick, lemon and cloves. Simmer for 10 more minutes. Remove from heat.

4. Using either tongs or two forks, dip the cookies for a few seconds in the warm syrup and place on cookie sheet to absorb the syrup. If the syrup gets too cold, gently reheat.

Sprinkle with chopped nuts and allow them to cool. These cookies keep very well and can be enjoyed for the next few days.

BAKLAVA

Recipe contributed by Christina Galanis Angelos

Most probably the most internationally recognized Greek dessert ,Baklava is a classic at all the Greek zaharoplasteia – pastry shops. Its origins can be traced back to various middle eastern countries, where it is usually made with pistachios, walnuts and almonds. In the Greek kitchen it is traditionally made with walnuts.

- *1lb butter, melted*
- *1 lb. pkg. filo dough pastry #4*
- *1 lb. walnuts, finely chopped*
- *6 Tbsp. sugar*
- *1 tsp. cinnamon*
- *¼ tsp. cloves*

Syrup:

- *4 cups water*
- *1 tsp. lemon juice*
- *2-3 whole cloves*
- *3 cups sugar*
- *1 cinnamon stick*
- *Slices of either a lemon or orange*

1. Combine the walnuts, sugar, cinnamon and cloves in a bowl and set aside. Melt the butter. Butter the bottom of a 9x13 pan. Place three filo pastry sheets in the pan, then brush the entire surface with butter. Repeat this 4 times. Spread 1/3 of the nut mixture over the top of the filo dough in the pan. Place another 6 sheets of filo, buttering in between each 2-3 sheet. Add another 1/3 portion of the nut mixture. Place the remaining filo sheets on top and butter each 2-3 sheets. Tuck the filo into the corners of the pan. With a sharp knife, cut the Baklava into even square pieces or into diamond shapes. Take the remaining butter (reheat if necessary) and pour evenly over the Baklava. Bake at 350 degrees for about 30-40 minutes. Cool completely and pour hot syrup over the Baklava. You can combine pistachios with the walnuts, or substitute completely for a variation.

2. Syrup: Combine all ingredients and bring to a slow boil while stirring. Reduce and simmer for about ½ hour. Pour the hot syrup over the Baklava. Syrup will thicken when cooled

HALVA

Recipe contributed by Julie Kokonis Phipps

- 1 cup canola oil
- 3 cups semolina (Melissa brand "Xovdpo"), or Farina may be substituted
- cooking spray
- a sprinkle of cinnamon before serving

Syrup:

- 3 cups sugar
- 4 cups water
- 1 tsp. vanilla extract
- 1 tsp. ground cloves
- 1 tsp. ground cinnamon
- 1 Tbs. freshly squeezed lemon

For people living in Greece during the Greek Civil War and the years of Reconstruction that followed, many goods were hard to come by. Olive oil was rationed, meat was very expensive and desserts were a luxury. In fact, in my Mother's family, other than "Xtipito avgo," (the yolk of an egg beat with 5 teaspoons of sugar till it turned into a frosting-like mixture to be eaten with a spoon,) "halva" was all the children were ever served. Of course, it was so delicious, they had no complaints! Today, the sweet aroma, grainy texture and smooth flavor of "halva" still make it a popular dessert in many Greek households.

1. Prepare the syrup first. Combine all the ingredients for the syrup in a saucepan over medium/high heat, stirring frequently until syrup boils. Allow to boil vigorously for 5 minutes. Remove from heat.

2. In a separate saucepan, heat the canola oil. Add the semolina, stirring constantly on medium heat with a wooden spoon until the mixture turns light brown. This is a very critical step that requires that you do not leave it alone or the semolina will burn and become bitter.

3. Turn off the heat. Put on cooking mitts and slowly and carefully, so as to prevent the hot oil from splashing, add the syrup to pot. The semolina will sizzle and bubble loudly. Turn the heat back on to high and stir the mixture until the syrup is absorbed (about 5-10 minutes). Remove from heat and cover the pot with a clean dish towel for 5 minutes.Spread mixture into a Bundt pan. Allow to cool. Then move onto a platter and serve.

KOULOURAKIA

Recipe contributed by Christina Galanis Angelos

- 1 lb. unsalted butter
- ¼ cup oil
- 2 ½ cup sugar
- 8 eggs
- 4 lbs. flour
- ¼ cup ouzo or fresh orange juice
- 1 tsp. vanilla
- 1 tsp. baking soda
- 6 tsp. baking powder
- 1 cup whole milk

Egg wash

- 2 eggs
- 2 tblsp water

If there is one dessert cookie that most young children learn to make next to their mothers side it is koulourakia. The dough is very forgiving, and it just begs to be made into different shapes. Traditionally it is made into the braided shape , as per the photo , and the fun is getting them to all look slightly uniform.

1. Beat sugar, butter and oil until fluffy. Add eggs one at a time. Add ouzo and vanilla.
2. Mix baking soda, baking powder and flour. Gradually add the flour into the butter mixture until the dough is soft and pliable. Take a small amount of the dough and roll into a strip about ½ inch x 8 inches. Make a braid or twist or circle.
3. Cover the unused dough so that it doesn't dry out. Place the twists about 1 inch apart on the baking sheet covered with parchment paper.
4. Beat 2 eggs and mix with 2 tablespoons water. Brush over the cookies. Bake in oven for 350º for 10-15 minutes, or until golden brown.

GALAKTOBOUREKO INFUSED WITH LEMON AND CINNAMON

- 6 cups 2% milk
- 1 cup fine semolina
- 1 cup sugar
- 1 cinnamon stick
- ½ a lemon – sliced with a peeler into strips – no pith
- 6 large organic eggs
- 1 tsp good quality vanilla essence
- 1 pkt filo pastry #4 - refrigerated
- 8 oz unsalted butter - melted – use a good quality European butter

Syrup:

- 3 cups water
- 2 cups sugar
- 1 cinnamon stick
- The other half of the lemon peel – not pith

Recipe contributed by Dimitra Alexakos

This classic dish can be found throughout Greece in the zaharoplasteia and is enjoyed slightly warm by the aficionados

1. Preheat oven to 350º.
2. Prepare the syrup first so it will be cool enough to pour over the cake. Place all the ingredients in a saucepan; bring to a boil stirring every so often, making sure the sugar has dissolved. Bring to a boil. Then reduce to a rolling simmer for about 10-15 minutes until it thickens slightly. Remove from heat and allow to cool without a lid.

To make the custard:

1. Place milk, semolina, sugar, cinnamon stick and the lemon strips in a saucepan. Stir constantly until the milk heats up and the custard starts to thicken. Use a wooden spoon to stir and be vigilant with this step or it will catch on the bottom of the pan and ruin the taste of the custard.
2. Once the custard thickens remove from the heat and stir it vigorously to cool down before adding the eggs. This allows as much steam to escape as possible.

3. Meanwhile lightly whisk the eggs and vanilla essence in a bowl to combine, when the custard mixture has cooled down, remove the cinnamon stick and the lemon strips then add the egg mixture to the custard and blend well.

4. Melt 8 oz unsalted butter and place to the side. Brush a 9x13 inch pyrex dish with butter place one piece of filo on the base of the dish , brush with butter , then place another 2 pieces of filo starting from the middle of the dish and overhanging either side of the dish (in an east west direction) then another 2 pieces of filo (in a north south direction) . then place another piece of filo folded in half on top of all the filo pieces – brush all the layers with butter.

5. Pour the custard mixture into the dish, then start the close the custard up by folding all the overhanging pieces of filo – starting with the last piece first so it does not tear. Again remembering to butter each layer as you bring it across the custard. Finally place another piece of filo across the top of the custard, this one will have to be folded in half –again remember to brush in-between the layers and tuck the edges down the side of the Pyrex with your pastry brush.

6. Brush the top filo sheet with butter and then dip your brush in cold water and brush across the top, this will give a nice sheen to the dish when it is baked.

7. Place a few slits with a paring knife so that the steam escapes. Bake for 45-55 minutes on the lowest rung of your oven, this will allow the base to cook through and the top of the dish will not brown too quickly. It is ready when the filo is a nice golden colour.

8. Remove from the oven allow to cool slightly then liberally pour the cooled syrup until it seeps through. This may have to be done in a couple of stages. Cut into squares or diamonds and enjoy.

RIZOGALO – RICE PUDDING

Recipe contributed by Georgene Karkazis Shanley

This creamy dessert is a favorite Greek pudding widely available in pastry shops and an easy recipe found in any Greek kitchen.

- 1 qt milk
- 3 oz rice
- 4 eggs
- 1/3 stick butter
- 1 cup sugar
- cinnamon

Melt butter in milk in cooking pot. Bring to almost scalding. Stir in rice and cook on simmer for 20 minutes until rice is cooked.

Add sugar and bring to boil over medium heat.

Mix eggs together and add some hot milk mixture slowly to the eggs – tempering the egg mixture – you do not want the eggs to curdle. Slowly incorporate all the egg mixture into the hot milk/rice mixture. Stir a little longer over low heat.

Pour into serving bowl and sprinkle with cinnamon.

VASILOPITA – NEW YEARS DAY CAKE

Recipe contributed by Julie Kokonis Phipps.

- 1 cup unsalted butter,
- 4 cups powdered sugar
- 6 eggs
- 4 ½ cups cake flour (Swansdown)
- 2 tsp. baking powder
- 1 tsp. baking soda
- Juice of 5 oranges
- Orange peel from 2 oranges
- 1 coin, wrapped in tin foil
- Slivered almonds or pomegranate seeds for garnishing (optional)
- Cooking spray

The vasilopita or the Sweet Bread of St Basil is steeped in immense tradition. It can be made either as per this recipe or as a yeast bread and decorated with elaborate braids

Cutting the "Vasilopita" on New Year's Day morning is an fun tradition Greek Orthodox families have been enjoying since the last half of the 4th century. The sweet orange flavor is a symbol of the sweetness of eternal life, as well as the hope that the New Year will be filled with the sweet joys of life, especially health and happiness. Typically, pieces of the cake are cut by the senior member of the family, the first piece for Jesus Christ, the next one for the Virgin Mary, then a piece for the parents and each child. Pieces can also be cut for the house, the church, or something else that is meaningful to the family. After everyone has been served his large piece of the cake, the table can become quite silent as the children devour their piece in search of the coin. The person whose piece has the coin is considered blessed and lucky for the year.

In the past, while most Greek families used a drachma as the coin for the cake, many wealthy families put in a gold lira worth several hundred dollars. While variations on this recipe abound, this tasty and authentic recipe comes from a local bakery "zaxaroplasteio" in the Athenian suburb of Kifisia.

1. Whip butter and powdered sugar for about ½ hour until fluffy. Add eggs, one at a time and combine well. Mix all the dry ingredients together. Add the dry ingredients, orange peel, and juice of the oranges to the mixture. Combine well.

2. Spray baking pan with cooking spray and dust with flour. Pour batter into a large, deep round metal baking pan (14 inch diameter, 3 inch deep)

DON'T FORGET TO ADD THE COIN TO BATTER BEFORE BAKING

3. Bake at 350° for about one hour. Allow the cake to cool completely in the pan before taking out and placing on a platter right side up. If you see that the coin fell out or stuck to the pan, simply stick the coin back into the cake. Sprinkle the cake with powdered sugar, using a sieve. Optional decorating ideas: outline the current year using the almonds or pomegranate seeds.

GREEK COFFEE

Recipe contributed by Dimitra Alexakos

- 2 small cups water
- 2 heaping tsp Greek style coffee
- 2 tsp sugar

There is an art form to making Greek coffee , long prized for its kaimaki (foam) top which everyone expects in their cup of coffee. Greeks will enjoy a coffee over a long period of time , discussing daily life and politics in many of the kafeneia that dot the proverbial Greek cities. A briki is best used to make the coffee. It is important to watch it carefully to ensure that it does not boil over – then you have lost the prized "kaimaki" or foam.

Place all the ingredients in the briki or similar small saucepan. Heat over low heat stirring occasionally to ensure the sugar has melted.

As the coffee mixture begins to rise inside the briki, remove immediately. Allow to subside and then place back on the flame again, for a second time. Once it rises a second time remove from heat. Then pour a little of the coffee in each cup to ensure some kaimaki will end up in each one. Then top off with the rest of the coffee.

FAVORITE RECIPES, MARGARITAS, VINAGRETTES AND AIOLIS - SARA MCKINNON MARTINEZ AND ANYA MARTINEZ

YUMMY MARGARITA RECIPES

PRICKLY PEAR MARGARITA- WATERMELON MARGARITA - JAPANESE CHERRY BLOSSOM MARGARITA - GINGER /LIME MARGARITA OR PINEAPPLE – GINGER MARGARITA

Prickly Pear Margarita

- 2 1/2 oz Voodoo Tiki Desert Rose Tequila - a prickly pear-infused tequila with a distinct flavor filled with sweetness and refreshing finish
- 1/2 oz triple sec
- 2 oz sour mix
- 1/2 oz orange juice
- dash of grenadine to color
- sugar coated lime wheel for garnish
- salt or sugar for rimming
- 1/2 oz triple sec
- 2 oz sour mix
- 1/2 oz orange juice
- dash of grenadine to color
- sugar coated lime wheel for garnish
- salt or sugar for rimming

Watermelon Margarita

- 1 1/2 oz tequila
- 1 oz triple sec
- 1/2 oz lime juice
- 1 cup seeded & pureed watermelon – run through a strainer
- 1 cup ice
- watermelon wedge for garnish

Japanese Cherry Blossom Margarita

- 2 oz sake
- 1 oz cherry syrup
- 1 oz sour mix
- 1 oz lemon juice (approx. 1 lemon)
- sugar for rimming
- cherry and lemon

Ginger/Lime Margarita or Pineapple – Ginger Margarita

- Juice from one lime
- 1 1/2 oz. Sauza Tres Generaciones añejo tequila
- 1/2 oz. Cointreau
- 3/4 oz. ginger-lime simple syrup

Ginger-lime simple syrup: Combine 1 cup peeled and sliced ginger, 1 cup fresh lime juice and 1 cup sugar. Bring all ingredients to a boil, simmer 2 minutes, let cool, then puree in a blender. Strain, and reserve liquid.
For salt rim: Mix together 1 part ginger powder, 2 parts Kosher salt.
Fill shaker with ice, tequila, Cointreau, lime and ginger-lime base. Shake. Pour into a rocks glass. Garnish with lime wedge.

Recipes contributed by SARA MCKINNON MARTINEZ

MEXICAN SHIMP & CRAB COCKTAIL

Recipe contributed by SARA MCKINNON MARTINEZ

- *3 pounds of cooked shrimp – deveined and cut in chunks*
- *1 cup of jumbo lump crab meat*
- *¼ cup chopped red onion*
- *¼ cup chopped cilantro*
- *2 tbsp. Diced jalapeno*
- *1 tsp. Horseradish sauce*
- *1 cup cocktail sauce*
- *¼ cup fresh lime juice*
- *2 avocados pitted and chopped (add just before serving)*
- *1 tsp. Hot sauce*
- *1 tbsp. Garlic powder*
- *Salt and pepper to taste*

Place all ingredients in a bowl, mix, cover and refrigerate for 3 hours - before serving fold in avocado. Garnish with fresh cilantro. Serve with tortilla chips. Very fun to serve in a martini glass

FAVORITE VINAIGRETTE DRESSINGS

HONEY-LIME VINAIGRETTE = MAPLE SYRUP AND SHALLOT VINAIGRETTE = HORSERADISH & GARLIC VINAIGRETTE = CITRUS VINAIGRETTE

Recipes contributed by SARA MCKINNON MARTINEZ

HONEY-LIME VINAIGRETTE

- ¼ Cup of fresh lime juice
- Zest of 1 lime
- ¾ cup olive oil
- ¼ cup apple cider vinegar
- 2 tbsp. Honey
- ½ tsp. Salt

MAPLE SYRUP AND SHALLOT VINAIGRETTE

- ¼ Cup maple syrup
- 1 shallot minced
- ¾ cup of olive oil
- ¼ cup apple cider vinegar
- ½ tsp. Salt

HORSERADISH & GARLIC VINAIGRETTE

- ¼ Cup of horseradish
- ¾ cup olive oil
- ¼ cup red wine vinegar
- 1 garlic clove minced
- ½ tsp. Salt

**optional: add plain Greek yogurt for a creamy dressing

CITRUS VINAIGRETTE

- 2 tbsp. Fresh orange juice
- 2 tbsp. Fresh lime juice
- 2 tbsp. Fresh lemon juice
- ¾ cup olive oil
- ¼ cup white vinegar
- ½ tsp. Salt

JALAPENO LIME VINAIGRETTE = MANGO VINAIGRETTE

JALAPENO LIME VINAIGRETTE

- ¼ Cup fresh lime juice
- ¾ cup olive oil
- 2 tsp. Minced fresh jalapeno
- 1/3 cup red wine vinegar
- ½ tsp. Salt

MANGO VINAIGRETTE

- ¼ Cup mango puree
- ¾ cup olive oil
- ¼ cup sherry wine vinegar
- ½ tsp. Salt

**optional – add fresh basil

JICAMA SALAD

Recipe contributed by SARA MCKINNON MARTINEZ

- 2 pounds of jicama, peeled and julienned
- ¼ cup of chopped cilantro
- 2 mangos sliced
- ¼ cup of fresh lime juice (add more if you like)
- 1 cup of fresh blueberries
- 1 cup of julienned carrots
- 1 tablespoons of honey (optional)
- 1 tablespoons of apple cider vinegar (optional)
- Salt & pepper to taste

1. Combine the jicama, carrots, cilantro, mango and blueberries.

2. Make the vinaigrette with fresh lime juice, honey and apple cider vinegar and salt & pepper. I often use only lime juice. You can also add orange or mango juice for sweetness. Toss together to coat. Refrigerate until ready to serve.

FAVORITE AIOLI'S

Be creative with aioli's – they are great drizzled over fish or chicken, in a fish/shrimp taco, on a vegetable or potato, as a dipping sauce and of course in a sandwich.
I love to put them in a squeeze bottle for a fun effect.

TRUFFLE AIOLI - GARLIC CHILI-LIME AIOLI - DIJON SAMBAL
VINAIGRETTE - DIJON SAMBAL VINAIGRETTE

Recipes contributed by SARA MCKINNON MARTINEZ

TRUFFLE AIOLI

- ¾ Cup mayonaise
- 1 tsp. Truffle oil
- ½ tsp. Garlic powder
- Pinch of salt

GARLIC CHILI-LIME AIOLI

- ¾ Cup mayonaise
- 2 garlic gloves minced
- 2 tbsp. Fresh lime juice
- ¾ tsp. Chili powder
- Pinch of salt

DIJON SAMBAL VINAIGRETTE

- ¾ Cup mayonaise
- 2 tbsp. Sambal or siricha hot sauce
- 1 tbsp. Dijon mustard
- Pinch of salt
- 1 tbsp. Diced chives

SESAME AIOLI

- ¾ Cup mayonaise
- 2 tsp. Sesame oil
- ½ tsp. Rice wine vinegar
- 1 tbsp. Toasted sesame seeds
- Pinch of salt

LEMONGRASS AIOLI - TEQUILA LIME AIOLI

LEMONGRASS AIOLI

- ¾ Cup mayonaise
- 1 tbsp. Mnced fresh lemongrass
- Zest of 1 lemon
- Pinch of salt

TEQUILA LIME AIOLI

- ¾ Cup mayonaise
- 2 tsp. Tequila
- Zest of 1 lime
- Splash of hot sauce
- Pinch of salt

CHILI VERDE PORK STEW

Recipe contributed by SARA MCKINNON MARTINEZ

- 2 tbsp. Vegetable oil
- 3 pounds boneless pork shoulder cut into 2 inch cubes
- ½ cup diced canned green chili peppers (anaheim)
- 2 cups of chicken stock
- 1 tbsp. Cumin
- 1 tbsp. Chili power
- 1 tsp. Cayenne pepper
- Salt & pepper to taste
- Sour cream – optional
- Toasted pepitas – optional

Season the pork cubes with salt & pepper. In a heavy Dutch oven, heat the oil on high heat, brown the pork until well browned. Add green chili peppers, chicken stock, cumin, chili powder and cayenne.

Cover and simmer on low for 1 hour stirring occasionally, until the pork is tender. Adjust seasoning if desired. Serve in a bowl with sour cream, cilantro and pepitas.

ANYA'S ISRAELI COUSCOUS SALAD WITH TZATZIKI SAUCEV

- *3 cups israeli couscous (cook couscous then chill with a drizzle of olive oil)*
- *¼ cup diced zucchini*
- *¼ cup peeepled and diced cucumber*
- *¼ cup diced tomato*
- *10 kalamata olives pitted and cut in half*
- *¼ cup cubed feta cheese*
- *¼ cup fresh lemon juice*
- *Salt & pepper to taste*

Refrigerate for an hour before serving. Then serve with a dollop of tzatziki sauce on top.

TZATZIKI SAUCE

- *2 peeled & chopped cucumber*
- *2 garlic glove rough chop*
- *2 tbsp. Fresh lemon juice*
- *½ cup of greek yogurt*
- *½ cup sour cream*
- *1 tbsp. Chopped fresh dill*

Recipe contributed by SANYA MARTINEZ

In a food processor or blender, combine yogurt, sour cream, cucumber, lemon juice, salt, pepper, dill and garlic. Process until well-combined. Transfer to a separate dish, cover and refrigerate for at least one hour for best flavor

ANYA'S FAMOUS GUACAMOLE

Recipe contributed by SANYA MARTINEZ

Mix well until smooth. Serve with tortilla chips

- 3 avocado's pitted and diced
- 2 tbsp. Diced red onion
- 3 tbsp. Diced tomato
- Salt & pepper to taste
- **optional – cilantro

RECIPES FROM XNIPEC RESTAURANT-MARIA LUISA ROMO

Maria Luisa Romo studied Communications Science and holds a master's degree in IT Administration but is also a crazy kitchen enthusiast. Everything changed when, over five years ago, her and her husband decided to take a different path in their professions. A business that they knew little about, but in retrospect left them invaluable gifts and new friends in the windy city. Her husband's family head the business now. For two years she has being collaborating for a Mexican enogastronomic magazine Saberadonde.com regarding topics surrounding the restaurant business and gastronomic themes of Chicago. Her and her husband have been recognized for their efforts to promote *Yucatecan* cuisine for the distinct magazine Gourmet Magazine, various works published in TimeOut Chicago, SunTimes, Chicago Readers, Chicago Tribune and for the second year in a row the Michelin Bib Gourmand Guide, to name a few.

#luisaromoCooks

THE BEGINNING OF NO END.

The idea of starting a restaurant was beyond my husbands and my career expertise and it was a way of life taken from the novel "*Pedro Páramo*". Where the dishes made us remember moments with our grandmothers, family reunions, the flavors of our homeland and at the same time savor one of the most common, ephemeral pleasures in life, eating and eating well.

Our beloved homeland, from my very particular point of view, can be divided culinarily into three dominant regions; the North, the Center, and the South. Each is distinguished for the syncretism derived from the colonization and indigenous cultures rooted in each region and historical moment. I admit that I am not a historian, nor an anthropologist specializing in the cuisine of my homeland, but I have had the fortune of enjoying the villages and listening to stories and family traditions of multiple generations and have tasted the dishes of the festivals and holidays. I have visited markets, where the cuisine reflects the character and personality of each region.

In the North region, you will hear find cold beer and flour tortillas in abundance. The majority of the strong dishes are made with meat. If we approach the coast, the magical simplicity of the seafood dishes predominates.

The central region's cuisine is complex in its ingredients, flavors, textures, and varieties of corn that are unimaginable. Vegetables are used in various forms (in desserts, beverages, or quesadillas) that are derived from desert plants to exotic decorative flowers. In some markets in the central region you can find insects, with or without legs, dried, or half alive, Xoconstles, (A type of prickly pear cactus), palm flower, squash flower, jicama flower and the most fresh and diverse vegetables cultivated in the area known as the lowlands "El Bajio". The capital (Mexico City) divides the north and south, and at the same time combines the best of both regions, and of the world. This cosmopolitan city offers an extensive variety of dining options.

The South, for its part, is marked by its heat and humidity that make the cooking techniques and the food itself as distinct as its many ingredients. The native tongues grace the names of some dishes of the peninsular zone and some insects are eaten dried as every day snacks in Oaxaca.

It would seem that we are speaking of many "*Méxicos*". Each region and each state's cuisine could fill an entire book. And without fear of being mistaken, there are not enough days in the calendar, to eat a different dish each day from each region of the country.

To attempt to translate all of this into a menu that reflects our Mexican heritage was not an easy task. To know the history and make it from scratch was more than enriching. It was trial and error; we grappled with uneasiness and bitter disappointments. To focus on a little known cuisine – Yúcatecan- in the Windy City, was a challenge. The work had to be done, executed, as well as administered, a project that, together with my husband was like another child that had to be raised with much time and little resources. And if that wasn't enough, add to it the non-existent business acumen.

The following chapter reflects in each dish a story and an anecdote of each one of the mixtures of flavors and culture with ingredients that are easily accessible in a city as diverse and rich as Chicago.

CHILES EN NOGADA – NOGADA CHILES

One of the most iconic dishes of the gourmet Mexican kitchen, without a doubt, are *Chiles en Nogada*. This dish appeared on the menu with the intention of celebrating the independence of Mexico.

It is a dish that is decadent for the eyes and the palate. The combination of fruits, cream and meat in a chile made it difficult to describe to first timers. Proudly, this dish has been the focus of attention of other culinary enthusiasts that reinterpreted it in their kitchens.

Undoubtedly, it is a seasonal dish thanks to its ingredients.

Originating from the central city of "Puebla de los Angeles", they were made by the nuns at the Augustine Convent of Santa Monica in 1821 to celebrate the recent signing of the treaties of Córdoba that granted independence to Mexico. Thanks to the patriotic fervor of the moment, the nuns decided to create a dish that was distinguished by the three colors of the national flag: Green, for independence; White, for faith and Red, for union.

6 servings

- 6 Poblano Chiles
- 1/2 pound of ground pork meat
- ½ pound of ground beef meat
- ½ cup of chopped almonds
- ½ cup of nuts
- ½ cup of raisins
- 1/2 cup of chopped apples
- 1/2 cup of chopped pears
- 1/2 cup of chopped peaches
- ½ cup of dried pineapple
- 1 bay leaf
- Two pinches of black pepper
- 3 garlic cloves very finely chopped
- 2 tablespoons of oil
- Salt

For the Nogada cream:

- -250 gr of cream cheese
- -3/4 cup of milk
- -1/4 cup of sugar
- -1/2 cup of almonds
- -1/2 cup of walnuts

For the topping:

- ½ cup of parsley fresh and dry, finely chopped
- 1 ½ cups of pomegranate seeds

1. Charbroil the *poblano chiles* in order to remove the skin and seeds.

2. Heat a frying pan with oil and when it's hot, add the finely chopped garlic. Before the garlic gets too dark in color, on a low flame add both the ground meats, salt and pepper. When the meat is half way done, add the chopped pine nuts and almonds. Mix everything together ensuring the meat has no clumps.

3. Add the chopped fruits and cover the pan for a few minutes. Allow everything to cook together for a few minutes stirring occasionally.

4. Stuffed the clean poblano chiles with the cooked meat and fruits.

5... Place the Nogada cream ingredients in the blender. Start with the cream cheese, sugar, almonds, and nuts and gradually add the milk. It should have a thick consistency and at the same time have a pleasant, nutty flavor, add sugar to taste.

To decorate the chiles

Pour some of the nogada cream on top of the chile and sprinkle the chopped parsley and pomegranate seeds on top.

Note: For the Nogada cream clean the nuts very well and boil them 3 minutes to avoid sourness.

Add more milk to the cream if not serving immediately because is tendency to get thick. More tips and how to prepare it. Follow me at #luisaromoCooks

POLISH-NACHOS

- *1/2 cup of chipotle sauce**
- *-1 1/2 cup of mayonnaise with lime*
- *-5 large potatoes*
- *-5 diced Smoked Polish Sausages. (Bobak's)*
- *-1/2 a white onion, diced*
- *-1 spoon of chicken flavor bouillon*
- *-1/4 teaspoon of black pepper*
- *-1 bay leaf*
- *-salt and olive oil.*

This dish has always caused a funny look with friends as an "appetizer fusion". This snack is inspired by the large Polish immigrant community that settled in the Windy City as a dominant community which has subsequently been replaced by the Mexican community in some areas. Without a doubt, Chipotle Chile is a very versatile ingredient. Although I must admit that this is not a dish that someone worried about their diet would eat, but it is a dish that, for its ingredients, satisfies all desires. On that same note, we prepared this dish as an entrée for a Polish wedding which was very well received. Served in a crusty flour tortilla chip making this dish a complete fusion of elements.

1. Blend the mayonnaise and chipotle sauce. Set it aside.
2. Cut in triangles the flour tortilla and fried in low heat to make nachos. Set it aside.
3. Cut the potatoes into small cubes and fry them over low heat with the Polish sausage, diced onion and the chicken bouillon. When the potatoes are soft, add the chipotle mayonnaise sauce. Add the pepper and bay leaf. The dish is ready when the fat from the mayonnaise sets. Add this on top of the nachos or on a flour tortilla.

You can add more or less chipotle sauce, depending in your tolerance to hot.

Buy the sausage here:http://www.tastesofchicago.com/category/bobak-sausage-company-maxwell-street-polish-sausage

CALABAZITA XNIPEC – SQUASH WITH XNIPEC SHRIMP

- 6 medium shrimps, raw (per squash)
- -4 round, small squashes – tatume-
- -1 large tomato (diced)
- -1/2 cup of sliced red onion
- -2 chopped garlic cloves
- -1/2 cup of annatto seeds or Sazón Goya with Coriander & Annatto (1 small packet)
- -Juice of 1 fresh orange
- - 1 teaspoon of white vinegar
- -1/4 teaspoon of oregano
- -1 unseeded and diced banana pepper –xcatic chile-
- -salt and olive oil.

One dish that has a complete combination of vegetable, seafood, and Yucatecan flavors is squash stuffed with Xnipec Shrimp. Xnipec shrimp have been on our menu as a classic and simple dish. On one occasion, one of our clients and later close friend wanted us to cater his wedding. While developing the menu, he suggested baby squash as a perfect dish that could be eaten in small portions

1. Boil the entire squash with salt. If you are using the large traditional Mexican squash, cut them in half and then boil with salt. Make sure the flesh is firm and remove the seeds.

2. Dilute the annatto seeds with the orange, salt, oregano and vinegar in a food processor or blender and set aside.

3. On low heat, sauté the tomato, onion, garlic and xcatic chile (banana pepper) in some oil. Season with the annatto seeds previously diluted or with Sazon Goya.

4. Slowly add the cleaned, raw shrimp.

5. Stuff the squash with the cooked shrimp and decorate with small pieces of parsley or cilantro. It can be served with tomato sauce to add a nice effect.

Goya with Cilantro & Achiote: http://goya.elsstore.com

Annatto seeds: http://www.myspicesage.com

- -3 Medium carrots. Diced and cooked
- -2 Big potatoes. Diced and cooked
- -8 unseeded Guajillo chilies
- -2 Garlic cloves
- -1 Pinch of oregano
- -1 Pinch of black pepper
- -1 / 4 teaspoon of salt
- -1 / 4 piece of medium onion
- 20 Tortillas
- 2 ½ cups of Canola Oil
- 1/2 teaspoon of salt

For the top

- -Chorizo
- -Lettuce
- -Sour cream
- -Fresh Mexican cheese
- -Chopped Onion

ENCHILADAS PLACERAS

One of the dishes that have been favorites between vegetarians and fans of enchiladas are the *Enchiladas Placeras*. From the state of Michoacan and very common in *"cenadurías"* (improvised street place to eat) and plazas in the city of Morelia where the frying guajiillo chile and chorizo aroma captivate many people. This dish can be vegetarian if you remove the chorizo sausage. It will not lose its originality because Guajillo chile is not spicy and very colorful.

1. Boil the potatoes and carrots. They should be cooked but firm. Let them drain.

For the sauce: Unseed the guajillo chiles and boiled with garlic until the chiles are soft. Blend the chiles with ¼ of the cup of the same water used for boiling. Add salt, pepper, garlic, oregano and onion to create the chile paste. The paste should be strained and sauté on low heat. Move constantly for few minutes. Set aside.

Vegetarian Enchiladas: Sauté potatoes and carrots with very little Guajillo sauce and set aside.

Traditional Enchiladas:1. Sauté the chorizo a couple of minutes. Add the potatoes and carrots. Add some Guajillo sauce to enhance the flavor if necessary. Set aside.

2. In another pan fry the tortillas for few seconds on both sides. They have to look firm but not hard or toast, move to a plate and cover with the sauce, friend them again.

3. Make an enchilada adding inside the tortilla onion and fresh cheese (Optional).

4. To serve: Place the enchilada in the final plate, garnish with chorizo, potatoes and carrots . Add fresh cheese, lettuce, minced onion and sour cream to finish.

To buy Chorizo spicy or non-spicy go to http://www.sigmafoodsusa.com

- *5 eggs*
- *-220 gr of cream cheese*
- *-1 tablespoon of vanilla extract*
- *-1 can of Evaporated milk*
- *-1 can of condensed milk*
- *8 large xoconostles*
- *-1 small cinnamon stick*
- *-Ground cinnamon*
- *-1 1/2cup of brown sugar*

FLAN NAPOLITANO DE XOCONOSTLE

Dessert is never missing in any story. And in this case, it is the union of two mixed cultures, distant, but very prevalent in my cooking the Yucatecan and the Otomi

By definition, flan is not a Mexican dessert. Its origins begin in Europe and as far as it is known, also as a savory dish. In the Peninsula, the dominant Flan Napolitano is more common, which is similar to cheesecake. For this occasion, I introduce some desert fruit such as Xoconostle (sour prickly pear), very common in the region of the Valley of the Mezquital-Hidalgo – and known as a crystalized fruit, salsa or even medicinal for curing cough and indigestion.

I admit that xoconostles are not easy to find, but the search is worth the effort. Their pink color and smooth, firm skin indicates when they are ripe.

1. Roast the Xoconostles with the skin on until the skin turns black. Remove the skin and seeds. Cut them into small pieces. Add water to level, cinnamon, and enough sugar (1/2 a cup) to make a syrup. Put aside.

2. In a sauce pan, caramelize the sugar over low heat stirring constantly until it turns a light brown color and the sugar is completely dissolved. Pour into the metallic mold used to bake the flan. Let it cool.

3. Blend the egg, vanilla, cream cheese, evaporated milk, and condensed milk. Pour the mixture into the mold with the caramel and the pieces of xoconostle in syrup prepared previously.

4. Cover and place in the oven inside of another pan with water so that the water covers up to ¾ of the molds with the flan mixture. Cover the dish well with aluminum foil to keep water from getting into the mixture and make sure there is enough water in the pan. Bake for an hour and a half at 350F or until a knife inserted into the flan comes out clean.

5. Allow the flan to cool to room temperature. Remove from the mold by using a knife to remove the flan from the edges of the mold. Turn the mold over onto a serving plate and decorate with some ground cinnamon

Tips: In Chicago you can find xoconostles in Mexican supermarkets such as El güero, La Chiquita, Cermak Produce. The best way to choose the xoconostle is the color –pink- and firmness.

VICKI'S HOLIDAY TRADITIONS–
VICKI PETERSON

VICKI'S BEST FUDGE EVER

- *3/4C (1&1/2 sticks) butter or margarine*
- *3 C sugar*
- *2/3 C evaporated milk*
- *1 pkg (12 oz. or 2 C) semi sweet choc chips*
- *1 jar (7 oz.) marshmallow creme*
- *1 C chopped nuts (optional)*
- *1 tsp vanilla*

This recipe is made in the microwave

1. Microwave margarine/butter in 4 qt. microwavable bowl on HIGH 1 minute or until melted. Add sugar and milk. Mix well.

2. Microwave on HIGH 5 min. or until mixture begins to boil, stirring after 3 minutes. Mix well, scrape bowl

3. Microwave on HIGH 5 1/2 stirring after 3 minutes

4. Gradually stir in chocolate chips until melted. Then add marshmallow creme, vanilla (and nuts) . Mix well.

5. Pour into greased pan. Cool. Cut and put into small dessert/candy cups or cut in slabs and give as gifts on a cutting plate with a cute cutting knife:)

HOT TIP.....Line pan with parchment paper and you can lift fudge out of pan and then cut......no dishes to wash.

VICKI'S SWEDISH NUTS

- 3 1/2 C plain shelled whole pecans
- 2 egg whites stiffly beaten
- 1 C white sugar
- 1/4 t salt
- 1/2 C butter

This recipe is actually from my sister Ginny who gave me a wedding shower gift that was a recipe box filled with all of her favorite recipes written on recipe cards...I still have not tried them all but this was a huge winner!!

Spread nuts in large flat pan. roast in 325 oven until light brown about 10-12 min. In large bowl beat egg whites until stiff. Beat in sugar and salt. Fold in roasted nuts. Melt butter in large jelly roll pan(that's a cookie sheet type pan with edges) Spread nut mixture over butter. Roast in 325 oven until all butter is taken up by nuts...about 30 minutes. Stir every 10 minutes. Transfer nuts to parchment paper or brown paper to cool. Delicous and a fancy treat!!

VICKI'S DIPPED WHITE CHOCOLATE PRETZELS

Melt white chocolate bark in microwave. (Melt white bark for 1 minute on high, stir, then do 30 second intervals in microwave until smooth and creamy.)Dip small twist pretzels or any shape in to white chocolate. Set dipped pretzels on wax or parchment paper. Before chocolate dries sprinkle decorative sprinkles or sugar on to pretzels. You do not have to submerge the entire pretzel in the chocolate dip. If just half or 3/4 of pretzel is dipped you will still have a very sweet and attractive treat!

VICKI'S PEPPERMINT BARK

This is really easy and amazingly impressive....Smash one package of candy canes in a plastic bag with a ballot or rolling pin. Melt one pound of white bark.(Check the label and anything made by Loghouse is really good white bark(white chocolate)....found at Target, Jewel, Walmart) Melt white bark for 1 minute in microwave on high....stir...then do 30 second intervals in microwave until smooth and creamy. Stir in peppermint pieces. Spread quickly on wax paper or parchment paper. Let harden the break into small pieces. If you want your bark to be "more pink" add a little red food coloring to melted chocolate.

BREAKFAST PIZZA

We start out every holiday waking up to the delicious aroma of the Breakfast Pizza baking in the oven. You can also use this recipe for lunch or dinner. From the breakfast pizza we move on to enjoy some Sweet Treats that are just some of my children's favorites and the recipes I have included are super easy!"

- 1 lb. pork sausage(I use the already cooked breakfast sausage links sliced)
- 1 pkg (8) refrigerated crescent rolls
- 1 C frozen loose packed hash browns thawed
- 1C shredded sharp Cheddar
- 1/4 C milk
- 5 eggs
- 1/2 tsp salt(optional)
- 1/8 tsp pepper
- 2 Tbsp grated parmesan

Brown sausage and drain or use precooked links sliced. Separate crescent roll dough into triangles and place on ungreased 12" pizza pan with points toward center. Press over bottom and sides to form a "pizza" crust. Seal perforations. Spoon sausage over crust. Sprinkle with potatoes and top with cheddar cheese. In a bowl beat eggs, milk, salt and pepper. Pour on to crust containing the toppings. Sprinkle with parmesan cheese. Bake at 375 for 25-30 minutes or until egg mixture is firm in center. Slice and serve and enjoy!! This is delicious!

Made in the USA
Charleston, SC
10 December 2012